Counselling The Abused *Christian Woman*

Counselling The Abused Christian Woman

A STEP BY STEP GUIDE

Laraine Birnie

COUNSELLING THE ABUSED CHRISTIAN WOMAN
A STEP BY STEP GUIDE

iUniverse books may be ordered through booksellers or by contacting:

iUniverse
1663 Liberty Drive
Bloomington, IN 47403
www.iuniverse.com
844-349-9409

All Scripture quotations, unless otherwise indicated, are taken from The Message/Remix. The Bible in Contemporary Language, Copyright © 2003 by Eugene H. Peterson. All rights reserved.

ISBN: 978-1-6632-5000-1 (sc)
ISBN: 978-1-6632-4999-9 (e)

Library of Congress Control Number: 2023901016

Print information available on the last page.

iUniverse rev. date: 01/27/2023

To the hundreds of emotionally abused women whom God has given me the incredible privilege of accompanying on their journeys to health and peace.

Contents

Acknowledgments

I would like to acknowledge the dedicated psychiatric help that my husband, Bill, provided to many of my clients. My daughter Carolyn introduced me to Elaine Aron's books on highly sensitive people. My daughter Sarah provided technical support and encouragement with getting this book published. And my friend Rod Wilson saw a book somewhere embedded in the first draught I sent him and provided excellent advice. God also used various difficult people in my life to give me the opportunity both to empathize deeply with my clients and to put into practice the strategies which I then suggested to them. It is my fervent hope that God will use this book to help more abused women move into the light.

Foreword

I t is a joyous occasion when you contribute an endorsement, reference, or foreword to support someone else's writing. Pleased for the author that the labour pains of writing have resulted in a birth, you join in his or her celebration and trust that this new life will have a significant impact.

But as I write these reflections, I am sad—sad because this book speaks to the experience of women who have suffered in unspeakable ways. These victims of various forms of violence— verbal, emotional, and physical—find themselves in a spiral of suffering that is hard to unravel. But the individuals referenced in this volume are a small fraction of the many partners, wives, and friends who have been or are being abused. Emotions are distant when exposed to impersonal statistics, but sadness is an appropriate response in the face of all this pain.

As a male who is a Christian, I also experience anger. The sociopolitical history of how men have treated women is arresting. When women are seen as less than human, men slip into attitudes that lack respect. When respect leaves the room, abuse flourishes, defenses strengthen, and women become victims. While men experience abuse in intimate relationships, the research suggests that my gender abuses more frequently. That makes me angry.

Sadness and anger become more pronounced when you realize that this book is not simply about abused women but about Christian women. Christianity is a faith tradition that has Jesus at its center—a man who became embodied, lived, died, and was resurrected, all with a profound sacrificial love for the sake of others. His existence was not egocentric but fully exocentric, focusing on the well-being of all humanity. Even casual readers of the Bible would notice that Jesus was not coercive or controlling, manipulative or abusive. And it was in His relationship with women, a group that sat on the fringes of society, where these qualities were most obvious. The ultimate contradiction is that many abusive men claim allegiance to the Christian faith.

Laraine Birnie speaks into this distressing area with clarity and credibility. Drawing on real-life examples from her years of clinical work, she paints a vivid picture of victims' lives while offering a hopeful road forward. In a world where faith is often disentangled from human experience, she is open about her Christian commitment without being preachy or disrespectful. This book is not only compelling for those struggling with abuse; it will also serve caregivers who offer healing both to the victims and the perpetrators.

—Rod Wilson, PhD,
author of *How To Help a Hurting Friend* and
Thank you, I'm Sorry, Tell Me More

Introduction

With God's help and the following ten-step guide, you can be an essential part of the healing journey for a Christian woman suffering emotional and psychological abuse. After a varied career, God led me to enter private practice, where I worked for almost thirty years with Christian women who were being emotionally abused by a partner, parent, family member, or employer. During that time, I developed a straightforward practical guide that can be used by lay counsellors, clergy, and other mental health professionals. My sincere hope and prayer is that in reading this book you will feel more confident in walking with abused women on their journeys to freedom.

While there are certainly men who are being emotionally abused in their relationships with their female partners, most are hesitant to acknowledge their situations and even less likely to come for help. Although my practice was essentially limited to Christian women, many of the strategies outlined can be used to help abused Christian men, especially when the abuse involves parents, friends, or employers. While my sessions included prayer and scripture, my guide is also relevant in working with individuals of other faith backgrounds, whom I also saw in my practice. This guide can also be easily adapted for online or telephone counselling. I have not gone into more depth with the biblical background material for understanding emotional abuse. For that I refer you to the excellent work of Michelle Donnelly in her book *Safe Haven: A Devotional for the Abused and Abandoned.* Many of the women that God brought to me had symptoms of anxiety or depression, but they also described problematic relationships which were hampering their recovery. This subset of caring, sensitive women had the misfortune to come from or currently be in very unhealthy personal relationships with their partners, parents, or others in their lives. Many of them reported being emotionally and psychologically abused. None of the women that I worked with reported being physically abused. In many ways, this made things more difficult for them, as they could not point to obvious physical signs of abuse, which are taken more seriously by friends, family members, and police. By using my guide as well as the many excellent resources already in print, I was able to help these women change the dynamics of their abusive relationships and embrace new hope. Once they understood their own personalities and their situations better and developed new ways of coping, many of the women were able to teach their abusive partners, family members, or employers to treat them with the respect that they deserved. Over the course of the sessions, many of their presenting symptoms were resolved, often even without medication, and it was heartening to see that many ended up teaching their friends or co-workers what they had learned. One of my clients worked in an office where her colleagues gathered around, eagerly awaiting news of what she had learned each week with me so they could try the strategies in their own lives. In some cases, my clients ended up sharing with other family members who were also being abused.

At the conclusion of counselling, almost all clients reported that they had attained respectful relationships with the previously abusive people in their lives and were confident that they could handle any future problems on their own. Women who had previously been tyrannized by a domineering spouse or difficult parent reported new confidence in terms of handling their "difficult person." Knowledge is power, and giving women more knowledge about themselves and their abusers allowed them to wrest control away from the abusers and become empowered themselves.

Above all, in working with these women, I needed to give them the love and support that they had often missed in their lives, and share with them my conviction that with God's help they could move to a new place of freedom to live and love fully.

Because of client confidentiality, the two fictional case histories I present in this book are just that. They are a compilation of the experiences of many different clients and represent a picture of the lives of many of the women I worked with. Some of my actual clients have kindly given me permission to share parts of their emails to me, and I include those here:

> I knew that my thoughts had become so jumbled and chaotic after a lifetime of head games from my mother I needed some guidance. So I reached out and was blessed to have Laraine as my guide through this mess in my head. It was

the best thing I ever did for myself. Not only did it help me put my thoughts in order, it gave me PEACE and best of all tools to cope going forward. (C. M.)

I'm thinking so much about how grateful I am for the help psychologically you gave me to get through this challenging time. I felt so alone before. Thanks be to God you were there. Miracles never cease when we have help such as what you gave me, to get me protected, aware and to have more faith. Thank you. (K. S.)

Therapy helped me see the true reality of my relationship with a narcissist. It gave me the opportunity to discuss my challenges and explore realistic options. I found it very helpful and honestly if you follow the advice in this book and put it into practice it can be life-changing. (G.C.)

Dr. Birnie is a talented, perceptive, empathetic therapist. She introduced me to the concept of narcissism and was instrumental in setting me on the path of recovery from my "fatal attraction" to narcissistic men. Her compassionate understanding, along with her ability to educate led me to a place of overcoming this devastating behaviour pattern. (D. H.)

Overview

E ach of the ten chapters represents a step in the process of working with a Christian survivor of abuse.

Chapter 1:   Determine whether the woman has any untreated clinical anxiety or depression that could hamper therapy.

Chapter 2:   Determine whether the woman is or is not a highly sensitive person.

Chapter 3:   Determine whether she is a survivor of emotional abuse and whether her abuser has a personality disorder.

Chapter 4:   Have her write and read aloud a confidential letter to her abuser.

Chapter 5:   Evaluate the relationship with her parents, and have her write letters to them.

Chapter 6:   Evaluate the healthiness of her church, friends, and employer.

Determine whether the woman has any
untreated clinical depression or anxiety
that would hamper counselling.

In my clinical practice, women often came to me initially with
symptoms of anxiety, depression, burnout, or stress, and my
first task was to make sure that if those symptoms had a medical
component, the women were being properly treated by a family
doctor or psychiatrist. If I determined that a woman was suffering
from an untreated clinical depression or anxiety disorder, I would
make sure that she was referred for the appropriate treatment.
I would explain to the woman that the work we needed to do
might be difficult at times and that I wanted to make sure that any
biochemical component of her symptoms was addressed. I would
not expect that a woman in the midst of an untreated clinical
depression or anxiety disorder would have the emotional strength
and energy to engage in counselling.

Once her clinical disorder was being managed medically, then my task was to help her deal with her difficult relationships. Medical treatment alone, while helpful, does not address the underlying stresses caused by ongoing difficult relationships, especially in the context of marriage or family. This was borne out by the fact that many women who were already receiving medical treatment for their anxiety or depression were still experiencing ongoing stress in their lives. In the first session, I would listen to the woman tell me about her problems. I would ask the occasional question, but primarily I would be listening to her account to determine whether to use my guide with her.

Let's begin with the first fictional case history—Marie.

ॐ

"Hello Marie," I said. "I notice that the letter from your family doctor says that she has prescribed Zoloft for symptoms of anxiety and depression; but she also says that you would like to talk to someone about stresses in your life."

"Yes." Marie nodded. "The Zoloft is helping me sleep better, and my appetite is back and my head is not so fuzzy, but I still feel anxious and stressed most of the time."

"What seems to be causing you the most stress?" I asked.

Well, to be honest, it's my marriage. I'm trying really hard to make things go well, but it's just not working, and I don't know what else to do to improve things."

"Tell me about it," I said.

"I know Steve is under a lot of stress," she said, "but he seems so critical of me, and nothing I do pleases him any more."

"How long have you been married?" I asked her.

"Well, it is about two years now." she added.

"And how was it at the beginning?" I asked.

"It was really amazing! I couldn't believe that he was interested in me, because I am pretty shy, but he always wanted to be with me. He would take me shopping, and he always wanted to pick out my clothes for me. He said that his mother had really good taste in clothes and he learned from her. I was a little hurt at first when he implied I didn't dress well, but he said that I was so beautiful that he just wanted me to look lovely all the time. We used to do so many things together. I wasn't really a fan of golf, but he insisted I try, so I did, and actually I was pretty good at it. I don't think he really liked that, so we stopped going so often. He started to accuse me of flirting with the other men, or with Dennis when he and his wife joined us for a round of golf. I have known Dennis for years, and we are just good friends, but after we would get home, Steve would start accusing me of wanting to have sex with Dennis, which was crazy. I love Dennis's wife, Shirley, and even if I thought about Dennis that way (which I don't), I would never do that to her.

"But he would go at me until I was practically in tears, and then the next day he would apologize and buy me something nice. When my parents first met him, they were really impressed because he took everyone out to this really expensive restaurant and paid for everyone. He and my dad hit it off, both being businessmen, but afterward my mom said she had a funny feeling about him. I was really annoyed, and she and I got into an argument. I am not that close to my mom, as I feel she always defers to my dad, so I didn't mind when Steve said he didn't think we should be spending that much time with them."

"What about your friends?" I asked.

"Well, it's funny you should ask," she added. "I used to have a few close girlfriends that I spent time with, but after I met Steve, he only wanted me to do things with him. I felt really flattered at first because he told me that we didn't need anyone else to be happy——just the two of us. He said he knew right from the start that he wanted to marry me, and he asked me about five times before I said yes. He wanted to have sex right away, and he gave me a hard time because I wanted to wait and be sure first.

"But back to friends. When I started to realize that I had been neglecting my friends and told him that, he got angry and asked whether he wasn't enough for me. I guess it was easier for me just to give in to him. He gave me wonderful presents, and he kept telling me how much he loved me. But whenever I wanted to do something with my friends, he would go into a sulk, so it wasn't worth it. After a while, some of my friends just stopped calling. I thought he would want to spend time with his friends, but he didn't, which I thought was a little strange.

"Another thing that bothered me was that he always wanted to know where I was and what I was doing. He would text me many times during the day even though he knew I was either at home or finishing my course. Sometimes I would be tempted just not to respond, but if I didn't get back to him right away, he would start phoning me to check in. I thought it was odd, because often I couldn't reach him and he would just say he was too busy to text me back."

"So it sounds like eventually it was just you and him?" I asked.

"Yes, and it wasn't that bad until I had little Stevie, our first baby. I was hoping that he would be with me in the hospital for the birth, but he didn't want to go to the prenatal classes, and then when I went into labour, he said he had an important meeting, so he wasn't there when Stevie Junior was born. I was so disappointed, but when I told him that, he just got mad and asked how I expected him to earn his salary if he just took off in the middle of the day. I thought his boss would have understood, but he said he didn't really like his boss, so he didn't ask.

"Anyway, things started to get worse after the baby was born. I was trying to nurse, and it was really hard at first, and he never offered to help with Stevie. In fact, he actually became more demanding and was angry if he thought I wasn't spending enough time with him. I tried to explain to him that infants take up a lot of time, but he just couldn't get it and kept at me for sex even when I was so exhausted that I could hardly function.

"Steve kept telling me that I had changed and I wasn't the woman that he had married, and it's true; I'm not. I'm a new mother, and my baby's needs have to come first. But he doesn't like it if I don't do what he wants right away. I try hard, but it seems the harder I try to accommodate him the more critical he becomes. He has even taken to going over to his mom's house for his meals more often. He says that at least *she* knows what he needs. His mom loves when he comes over, and she always cooks his favourite food. She doesn't really like me because before we got married Steve was over at her place all the time, and now he isn't. When I complain about it, he says it is because his mom is always happy to see him and I'm not. And that's true, because sometimes I am frustrated that he doesn't offer to help with little Stevie and I feel like he is doing me this big favour when he just holds him long enough for me to catch up on chores.

"He is always commenting on the fact that his mom's meals are so delicious and saying that he wishes that she could teach me how to cook because she took some Julia Child cooking course."

"How do you get along with his mother?" I asked.

"Not great," Marie responded. "I think that she really didn't want Steve to get married because she was always the most important woman in his life. When I first met her, she showed me a photo album of Steve which had all these photos of his ex-girlfriends that she thought he was going to marry. Some looked like models, and I felt really ugly by comparison. She always bragged about Steve and told me she was sure that whoever he married would be wonderful, but I got the feeling she didn't really mean me.

"I thought she would be really interested in little Stevie, but she only came to visit us once, and then she kept asking us to come over to her place. It is just so hard to lug a newborn anywhere without taking half the house with you. And it is not like she is that far away. In fact, she seems okay to drive all over town to visit her friends. I was really hoping that she would be a help to me after Stevie was born, but she just never was."

"That must have made you sad," I added.

"More angry than sad," said Marie. "I always thought that a man's first responsibility was to his wife, but Steve says that his mom is really important to him, especially since his dad died. It is just that she is always asking him to come over and fix something for her, and he just jumps when she calls, whereas if I ask him to do something, he gets really annoyed and accuses me of being 'high maintenance.'

"I am so confused because when we first met, he always wanted to do everything with me and was annoyed if I met my girlfriends occasionally, whereas he will spend three or four evenings over at his mom's now. I get that it is easier for him over there—no baby crying or having to change diapers—but that is what parenting is all about. Sometimes I think that he doesn't really want to be a parent. He just wants me to continue to meet his needs without having to do anything about meeting mine."

"What about your own parents?" I asked.

"Well, that was disappointing too," Marie replied. "I guess maybe I was expecting too much from them too. After Mom and I had that argument about Steve, we didn't see them that much, but I hoped that after the baby was born they would come around.

"The problem really is my dad. I mean, I love my dad, but he rules the roost and my mom just goes along with whatever he wants. He says he is not into babies, and he does have a pretty busy life with his investment business and his hobbies. He always wants my mom to be available 24-7, so she doesn't have much of a life outside the marriage. He used to treat me okay, especially when I started out taking business courses, but when I changed over to interior decorating, he stopped asking me about my courses and didn't want to hear my ideas. He said I was making a big mistake not going into business like he did. He did like Steve, though, and they got along okay at first, but then Dad said he thought Steve was arrogant. That was a joke, because Dad is always bragging about his work and how important it is. My mom just sits there and nods and smiles at him. I just try not to roll my eyes.

"Anyway, I thought at least Mom would want to come over and spend time with the baby, but she said that Dad didn't want her driving the car by herself, and of course he was at work all day. I think she might have been more involved if Dad encouraged her, but she doesn't seem to have a mind of her own. She lets Dad make all the decisions. I told her that Steve could drive over and pick her up, but she said she didn't want Dad to be upset if she wasn't back in time to make his supper. It would be different if she had other grandkids to look after, but it is just me. Anyway, they do send lovely gifts for Stevie, so I guess I should be happy about that."

"Has anything else changed lately with Steve?" I ask.

"Well, now that you mention it, he spends a lot of time on the computer down in our rec room. When I ask him what he is doing, he always says it is work, but whenever I come into the room, he always shuts it down really quickly so I can't see the screen. I have wondered if he is into pornography, but of course he denies it and tells me I am crazy.

"He is pretty forgetful but blames it on me if his things go missing, so I try to remember where he might have put his things just so I don't get criticized. I just don't know why things have changed and why he seems so difficult to be around or even have a conversation with. We go to church, and he is always reminding me that I am supposed to be submissive and that he is the head of the house, but there are Bible verses about the husband loving the wife, and he doesn't talk about those. Our pastor is big on the husband having spiritual leadership in the home, but Steve doesn't read the Bible or even pray; he just tells me what I am supposed to do. I know I am rambling on, but it feels good to just talk to someone about my struggles.

"I know it must be my fault, because he can be wonderful to other people, and most people tell me I am so lucky to have such a handsome husband. I guess I was taken in by his good looks; I figured someone that good-looking wouldn't pay attention to me.

"I think the thing that bothers me the most is that he thinks he is always right. Every time I have a different opinion, he rants on about how I am so stupid and how I don't know anything. I did go to university, but he makes me feel that I am nothing.

"I guess that is part of why I am feeling down. The medication that Dr. Smith gave me helps a little, but I just feel like I am alone in this marriage and I can't trust him to be there for me if I really need him."

"Has there been a time when you really needed him?" I asked.

"Yes," Marie said. "When my sister died last year, I really wanted him to be able to support me emotionally, but he just couldn't put himself in my shoes. He was even annoyed when I wanted him to look after Stevie so I could go to the funeral. He told me I should have called our babysitter, but it was the weekend and she wasn't available. He was okay for a few hours that day, but at night it was like he thought I should get over it and pay attention to him again. It is hard for me to admit that I can't really share anything important or emotional with him, as he just doesn't get it.

"Maybe I am just too sensitive. He is always telling me that, and maybe he is right. I end up worrying about things, and I do take things to heart. I wish I could let things roll off my back like he does. It is just that things seem so unfair at times, and I do get more emotional when I feel that no one really understands me.

"I have talked to my doctor and my pastor, and they both know Steve and think he is wonderful, so I don't think they believed me when I told them how I feel. And it is true that every now and then Steve seems like he really cares about me; he will bring me flowers or chocolates and tell me he loves me.

"I feel bad saying this, but sometimes I think he does that because he just wants sex. If he has been really critical of me all day, I just can't get in the mood to have sex, and he thinks I have a problem in that area too.

"Anyway, Steve and my pastor both think I need to get therapy to deal with my issues, so that's why I am here. I know there must be something I am doing wrong; otherwise, my marriage would be better. I see other couples in the church, and they all look so happy together."

"Have you tried marriage therapy?" I asked.

"Gosh no!" Marie added. "I told Steve we should go for counselling, and he just said that he wasn't going to pay good money to have some dumb counsellor tell him what to do. He said that I was the one with the problem so I should go by myself. I hope you can help me figure out what I need to do to make things better in my marriage."

"Well, Marie," I said, "I work with women short term—usually six to eight sessions, meeting every two weeks, and I will be your guide, helping you to understand yourself and Steve better. Sometimes this work can be challenging, so I want to tell me if we are going too fast or if you are feeling any anxiety. Usually, I will give you homework to do in between the sessions. I am looking forward to helping you feel better about yourself and your situation, and I trust that God will show me what I need to do to help you. Do you mind if I pray with you before we end?" "That would be great," Marie said.

⚜

This first session with Marie raised some red flags for me in terms of how her husband was treating her, as well as her relationship with both her parents. There was no evidence in Marie's narrative to suggest that her husband was suffering from depression, anxiety, or PTSD, all of which can result in emotional abuse or neglect. On the contrary, he was doing well in his job, seen positively by people outside the family, and was not using drugs or alcohol. The main features she described were those of someone who appeared to be critical, jealous, controlling, and self-absorbed, as well as quite demanding that his needs take precedence over those of his child. These initial red flags were indicators to me that it might be worthwhile to explore whether he had some unhealthy personality traits. There were also red flags in terms of how she described her mother and father, which would need to be addressed later.

Regarding Marie herself, she was already on medication, so any biological component was being treated. She raised the issue herself of her sensitivity, and so I would begin with that in order that she could have a better understanding of herself before we tackled her marital relationship.

*Determine whether the woman is or is
not a highly sensitive person (HSP).*

I t is important to determine whether a woman fits the criteria
for a highly sensitive person in the early stages of counselling,
as such individuals experience more difficulty with problematic
relationships. This is especially true of many Christian women
who have been told to just pray and be supportive of their
husbands, with assurance that God will honour that.

I used the checklist developed by Elaine Aron in her book
The Highly Sensitive Person. This checklist is available to the public
online at her website at https://hsperson.com. For reasons I didn't
fully understand at first, a large percentage of emotionally abused
women in my practice turned out to be what Aron labels as
"highly sensitive people." These people make up only 15 per
cent to—20 per cent of the population and have unique gifts and
challenges when it comes to their personal relationships.

I wanted to discover at this early stage whether our fictional Marie fit the criteria for an HSP.

"Hello, Marie," I said. "I noticed that you mentioned that you thought you were 'too sensitive' and that maybe that was contributing to your problems in your marriage. Elaine Aron has written a book called *The Highly Sensitive Person*, and she describes people whom others might label as overly sensitive. I will highlight a few of the things that she talks about today, and then I will get you to go to Elaine Aron's website and take the test yourself.

"According to Elaine Aron, highly sensitive people are much more in touch with their emotions than most people. They process emotions more deeply, are more bothered by injustice, often find social interactions tiring, and often feel misunderstood by the people around them. They may be told they are 'too sensitive,' whereas the reality may be that the other 80 to 85 per cent of people around them are not particularly sensitive. These non-HSPs (being the majority in the population) believe that their responses to the world are the correct ones, and certainly they are the most common ones. But they can inadvertently make the highly sensitive person feel odd, weird, or too reactive. Some women have told me they have believed they were crazy because things bothered them that others would just brush off. The sensitivity can be to physical things like scratchy clothes and temperature, or to their emotions, which they have often learned to downplay rather than be subjected to criticism by others.

"Highly sensitive people are great in occupations of service, the arts, or healing professions, as they give 110 per cent to what they do. The non-HSPs are better suited to tougher occupations, like ER medicine, the military, firefighting, and politics. Highly sensitive people don't need many friends, but they do need at least one person who understands them. Because they are not in the majority in North American culture, it is often hard for them to find others who think and feel the way they do. North American culture also tends to reward aggression and competition, so highly sensitive people are often not valued, especially if they find themselves in the wrong profession. Is any of this sounding familiar to you, Marie?"

"Wow, that sounds so much like me I can't believe it. Not just Steve but my dad was always telling me I was too sensitive and to 'toughen up,' as he put it. My mom always had to cut the labels off my clothes because they were too scratchy, and I used to cry easily if someone got hurt or treated badly.

"I hated loud noises and big crowds, and it was hard to find friends who weren't always teasing me about being too shy or a worrywart. I used to get really upset when I thought things were not fair in games or even when Mom and Dad were being unfair. My sister, Bonnie, was just the opposite. She was a tomboy and teased me a lot. But my brother John was more like me, and he and I used to hang out when we were younger because he liked music and was always playing his guitar.

"I found it hard in high school when everybody was dating and making out and I just wanted to get home early and go to bed. My first boyfriend dumped me because he said I was no fun to be with, but I just couldn't take the high energy of crowds for very long."

"Did your mom understand you?" I asked.

"Definitely more than my dad," Marie replied, "but I think she was sensitive too, so she wasn't able to do much to protect me. One of my teachers told my mom that she didn't think I would make it through university unless I toughened up more."

"Well, Marie, I would like you to take the test yourself, and we can talk about it some more the next time we meet."

In the next session, Marie revealed that she scored a twenty out of a possible twenty-two on the HSP test, indicating that she was a very highly sensitive person.

"So Marie," I said. "It turns out that you are a very highly sensitive person, as you scored higher than 90 per cent of people who take this test. It is important that you understand that you have a uniquely sensitive emotional makeup that has wonderful assets but also liabilities. Because you have a heightened sensitivity to other people and their moods, you need to be especially wise in terms of protecting yourself from unhealthy personal relationships with parents, your partner, and even friends and colleagues."

"Does that mean I am weird?" Marie asked.

"Not at all," I said. "It just means that your brain and nervous system are more finely tuned than those of most other people, and you will be more prone to anxiety or depression if you are not in an emotionally supportive relationship. Highly sensitive people take things more personally and feel things more deeply, so they are more likely to suffer emotionally when in an abusive relationship. Being a highly sensitive person means you won't just bounce back when wounded emotionally and you need to take special care to protect your emotions."

"I guess that explains why the things that Steve does bother me so much. But maybe Steve is right and the problems are all my fault."

"That's not true, Marie," I added. "Steve's behaviour towards you is still disrespectful, regardless of whether you are highly sensitive or not. It just means that the impact of his behaviour on you is more powerful than if you were not so sensitive.

"I wish I could change who I am and not be so sensitive," Marie said.

"But God created you perfectly, and your sensitivity is a wonderful asset in so many ways," I replied. "It makes you a wonderful mother, tuned in to your child, and you are conscientious and a good friend to others and can feel things deeply. Your sensitivity enables you to develop your artistic talents and to have deep empathy for other people who are hurting."

"I guess it is a relief to know that I am not the only one like this," Marie added. "I think you are right that even if it is harder sometimes to be a highly sensitive person, I wouldn't trade who I am. It is good to know I am not weird or crazy like Steve says. And it was helpful to read in Elaine Aron's book about how society needs people like me to balance the other folks who are not as sensitive. I guess I never really thought of my sensitivity as an asset before."

⚜

We will return to Marie often in this book, but I want to introduce you to another fictional woman, Stella, whose personality and history are different from Marie's and will illustrate a different outcome.

Stella was an attractive middle-aged office worker whose children were older and whose husband was currently employed in a sales office. She worked with Marie's husband, and Marie had mentioned that she was seeing me when they met at an office party. Stella was not clinically depressed; nor did she have an anxiety disorder. She had been married for twenty-five years to a man she described as "very self-centred."

In our first session, Stella said, "Marie and I were just sharing our frustration with our respective husbands, and she was telling me about this highly sensitive person test. To be honest, I don't think it applies to me. I did the test, and I only scored a four."

"That's interesting Stella," I said. "Let me explain a bit more about people who are not highly sensitive. To start with, they can often have easier lives. Because they are not as tuned in to the emotions of the people around them, they are often able to ignore or tune out more of the bad behaviours of their partners. They can let things roll off their backs more easily, and they don't take things as personally. Their emotions can withstand more stress than those of the highly sensitive person, and their moods are not tied in to those of other people as much. Because they are able to tolerate higher levels of stress without getting overwhelmed, they can function well as ER physicians, firefighters, and corporate CEOs. They tend to do well in positions of leadership. But the downside is that often they are not aware that they may be insensitive to other people's feelings and inadvertently step on people's toes. They are not caught up in worrying about what others think of them and so can be more independent in their decision-making.

Because they are the majority in North American culture, they usually don't suffer from feelings of inadequacy or worry about whether they fit in. They may have some areas in which they are sensitive, but overall they are more robust in terms of their personalities.

"Is any of this sounding familiar to you Stella?" I ask.

"Yes it is" she added. "I think I have always been a strong person, and I enjoy being on a deadline with work. I would often stand up to my boss if I thought he was being unfair. My family sometimes told me I was insensitive, as I would seem to gloss over things that were important to them or make comments that they thought were rude. I tended to work better with men than women, as I didn't like to beat around the bush. I think sometimes women didn't like me because I was too direct, but men were okay with that. I tend to manage okay in emergencies, as I don't panic or get overwhelmed. I was never very sensitive about foods, strong smells, or scratchy clothing, and I am not bothered by our neighbour who tends to mow his lawn in the early morning hours. I guess in some ways I am usually able to go with the flow."

"That is interesting, Stella. Many non-HSPs end up spending longer in abusive situations before going for help because they can tolerate the abuse and don't take it as personally. The downside is that they may not take the appropriate steps to hold an abusive person accountable if it doesn't bother them as much.

"Maybe that is why I have stayed in my marriage so long." Stella added. "It has been twenty-five years, and I am finally getting fed up with my husband's behaviour.

"I think that is likely the case Stella," I said.

As noted above, there are assets and liabilities with sensitive and non-sensitive people; however, the majority of women in my practice were highly sensitive people. It would seem that these individuals are more likely to suffer anxiety and depression because of their emotional makeup and are therefore more likely to see a counsellor for help when they are in difficult relationships.

Many of the HSPs in my practice were also more likely to self-examine and blame themselves for their relationship problems, and thus suffer more unwarranted guilt when things went wrong. It would appear that HSPs both need and benefit from counselling more than the non-HSPs (the less sensitive women).

3

Determine whether she is a survivor of emotional abuse and whether her abuser has a personality disorder.

"Emotional abuse involves controlling another person by using emotions to criticize, embarrass, shame, blame or otherwise manipulate them."[1] Many women believe that abuse is limited to physical or sexual abuse and so do not see their partners' interactions as being abusive. This is often true of Christian women who have been told that the Bible says that the husband is the "head" of the wife and so is entitled to tell her what to do. An excellent expository of Ephesians 5 may be found in John Temple Bristow's book *What Paul Really Said About Women*. Bristow notes that when Paul talks about the husband being the "head" of the

---

[1] Sherri Gordon, "What Is Emotional Abuse?" Verywell Mind, August 8, 2022, https://www.verywellmind.com/identify-and-cope-with-emotional-abuse-4156673.

wife, he is not using the Greek word "*arche*" (from which we get "archbishop"), meaning "In charge of someone, or superior to." Rather the apostle Paul uses the Greek word "*kephale*," which refers to a captain who goes out in front of his wife and children in battle to protect them from harm.

It is clear that the biblical example for the husband's headship is Christ, who laid down his life for us rather than lording it over us. The Christian husband is told to love his wife as Christ loved the church, so there is no place in Christian marriage for disrespect, harshness, manipulation, or emotional abuse.

In Ephesians 5, Paul also encourages the wife to "respect" her husband and support him voluntarily. It will be natural for a wife to voluntarily "submit" to (i.e., respect and support) her husband if he is truly loving her. If, however, the husband tries to enforce submission, then it becomes subjugation and abuse and is no longer voluntary on the part of the wife. Prior to the specific instructions to husband and wife, Paul encourages all people to "submit" to one another, so it is not just a specific injunction to wives (Ephesians 5:21 MSG).

Failure to identify emotional abuse can result in a woman lying to herself that she can handle it or that it is not really that bad. It is important that she recognize the seriousness of her partner's abusive behaviour and acknowledge that despite all her efforts to date, she cannot change the pattern. Most people want to believe that they can change the situation by their own efforts, prayers, or tactics. Most of the survivors of abuse that I have worked with have been extremely strong, faithful, optimistic women who believe that they must hang in with their bad marriages no matter what. Unfortunately, this belief has often been fostered to a greater extent within Christian circles where there is an expectation of forgiveness and the extension of grace to the abuser. Some of the women that I worked with were told by their pastors or elders to just submit to their husbands and pray for him and things would get better. To be fair, some pastors did try and hold the abusive husband accountable for his behaviour, but in many cases, it was a futile effort. Sometimes when a woman was brave enough to share the abuse with her pastor, the focus became one of "helping" the abuser rather than looking to support the woman. Again, that may be a reflection of the fact that many church leaders do not have the skills to help an emotionally abused woman and so they focus on trying to hold the male abusers responsible instead. Often their approach is one of offering extended counselling sessions with the abuser but, unfortunately, ignoring the abused woman's needs.

For many abused women, their own focus has been on trying to change their abusers' behaviour by adapting various new strategies themselves. This gives them the illusion of power and control. The wife may believe, "If only I could be a more loving partner, then he wouldn't treat me so badly."

The reason this is a hopeful strategy and one that the woman holds on to is that she thinks that if she is the problem, then she can fix it. If she is not the problem, then she believes there is nothing that she can do, and that is too depressing for her to admit.

While this misplaced hope that she can change things can be comforting to the survivor and keeps her hanging in, it prevents her from seeing the reality that she cannot actually control her abuser. Ironically, in order to heal the woman must first give up hope—unrealistic hope, that is. She must let go of the hope that if she figures out how to meet his needs, he will stop abusing her. So how can we help the abused woman to relinquish this hope and identify herself as being emotionally abused? There are numerous excellent resources, such as *The Verbally Abusive Relationship* by Patricia Evans, which I encourage women to read at this stage.

For many years, I was puzzled by the fact that many abused women felt guilty or ashamed and blamed themselves for the unhealthy relationship. But I came to understand that guilt and responsibility are two sides of the same coin. If I am the guilty one, then I can work to change my own behaviour. However, if the other person is the guilty one, then I can't do anything about it, and since I am not responsible for the abuse, I must give up hope of changing it. That thought is often too depressing for a woman in an abusive relationship, so she holds on to the belief that there must be something she can do (or not do) to change things. Believing that she is the guilty one (i.e., the one with the problem) gives her hope for change in the future.

In this context, it is important for women to understand the difference between true and false guilt (or shame). We want people to feel guilty when they have acted in a hurtful, mean way toward someone else, because then that guilt will trigger an apology and an attempt at restitution. However, false guilt, or shame, is the result of something that someone else does to us in order to manipulate us to meet his or her needs and make him or her happy. If a woman has been conditioned from childhood to believe that it is her job to make her parents (and subsequently her partner) happy, then she will feel responsible for their happiness. Unfortunately, unhealthy people are only too ready to blame their partners for their own unhappiness. The belief that it is her responsibility to make others happy is a false belief that will be tackled later in the guide.

By the time the woman had read about the different types of emotional abuse and we had discussed it more fully, she usually had an awareness that her situation did not represent what God set forth as a normal marriage. Again, because Christians are often reluctant to share about their difficult marriages, she may have felt that her situation was too embarrassing to share with others. At that point I needed the woman to understand that she was feeling stressed because she was experiencing emotional abuse.

Obviously, some instances of emotional abuse can be the inadvertent result of a partner or parent having untreated depression, an untreated anxiety disorder, or PTSD. A partner who suffers from depression is likely to be emotionally neglectful, as he is using all his energy just to manage his own emotions. This may explain why he is unable to take the focus off himself and meet her emotional needs. In those cases, the woman needs to encourage her partner to go for help, and once a diagnosis is made and treatment is initiated, her partner may well be able to handle his irritability or anxiety more appropriately. However, in general, the women in my practice were much more likely to report that their partners were very pleasant with other people, functioning adequately in their work and social lives, but were subjecting them to considerable emotional abuse in their private lives.

I want to address the terms "diagnosis" and "personality disorders," as these can be confusing for a Christian reader. The purpose of making a diagnosis in medicine is so that an appropriate treatment plan can be instituted. Your doctor needs to make a diagnosis of an infection so you can be given the proper medication. Similarly, in psychiatry and psychology a diagnosis guides the treatment. A diagnosis of depression warrants a course of antidepressant medication, just as a diagnosis of diabetes warrants a course of insulin.

In psychiatry there is a group of mental illnesses called personality disorders, and if that diagnosis is made, then the counsellor has a better idea of what will or won't be helpful in terms of treatment. At this stage in the counselling, I would take time to explain to the woman in more detail about personality disorders. Persons who are not capable of changing their thinking or behaviour are said to have personality disorders because they have fixed unhealthy views of themselves, other people, and the world around them. Psychiatrists have broken down the personality disorders into different subgroups which are listed in the *Diagnostic and Statistical Manual (DSM-5)*. This manual is used by psychiatrists and psychologists to diagnose the various types of mental illnesses. The information about personality disorders is now easily accessible to the average person at the Mayo Clinic website (https://mayoclinic.org). The most common personality disorder that the women who came to me uncovered in their spouses was narcissistic personality disorder. Fortunately, the percentage of individuals with this disorder is small (no more than 6.2% according to the DSM-5, but 50 per cent to 70 per cent are males). However, the emotional damage that they do to those who have relationships with them is incredible. The suffering that they cause their partners, wives, children, or employees is so extensive that most people in any kind of relationship with these narcissistic individuals end up seeking counselling.

Individuals with narcissistic personality disorder will sometimes come to a counsellor if their partners force them, but they are incapable of seeing their own roles in any relationship problems. They have been known to convince naive counsellors that they are the victims, as they will portray themselves as charming, helpful people who don't understand why their partners are upset with them. If seen individually, they may also use a counselling session to vent their frustrations but will generally remain only as long as the counsellor doesn't challenge their thinking or suggest that they make any behavioural changes. These individuals can take up an inordinate amount of time with pastors or naive counsellors who do not understand the limitations of individuals with personality disorders to make any meaningful changes. In general, however, the narcissists are less likely to come for counselling and less likely to benefit from it given the constellation of symptoms they display.

There are some psychiatrists and psychologists who do work directly with individuals with personality disorders, but they are in the minority, as it is a lengthy process with limited gains even if the person is willing to come for therapy. Some psychiatrists have speculated that these narcissistic individuals actually have a deep sense of shame and that their behaviours are attempts on their part to convince themselves and others that they are special people.

To discover whether a woman in an abusive relationship was possibly dealing with a narcissistic personality, I would tell her that I was going to describe some traits of people with narcissistic personality disorder to see if this rang any bells in terms of her husband.

I would then explain that narcissistic individuals can't seem to put themselves in another person's shoes or see another person's perspective. They never concede an argument, as they believe that they are always correct. They also never apologize because they don't see the impact of their abusive behaviour on their partners. They have one set of rules that they expect everybody else to abide by and a different set for themselves. They need more than the average amount of praise and admiration and will brag about their skills and lie and manipulate with ease. They can play the victim in a heartbeat if they think it will get them what they want. They have a sense of entitlement, believing that others should always meet their needs, but they don't see that they should reciprocate. They believe their behaviour and attitudes should never be questioned or criticized.

The mood swings of men with narcissistic personality disorder correspond with whether or not the women they are with meet their needs. But they are bottomless pits, so no matter what the women do, it is never enough. By the next day, such a man has forgotten every sacrifice she has made. Men with narcissistic personality disorder really can't do marriage, which requires a depth of emotional intimacy that they are incapable of giving. In parenting they can't do agape, or self-sacrificing love. They can do casual friendships (if the friends are not demanding), but they can't put another person's needs ahead of their own unless there is something in it for them. They also can be a huge problem for colleagues in the workplace because they really don't view other human beings as deserving respect.

Because these unhealthy individuals can interact normally with outsiders, the woman is rarely believed when she tries to share her experience with friends or family. This is compounded if the abuser has a position of some authority in the church. Women in relationships with men who have narcissistic personality disorder will often describe their incredulity that these men can appear to be so loving and attentive with other people but completely neglectful of them. Because their partners constantly deny their complaints and insinuate that they are crazy (gaslighting), these women end up questioning their own reality. This, coupled with the fact that the women are rarely validated in their community, also contributes to their distorted belief that it is all their fault.

As I highlighted the narcissistic traits, I would note whether the woman I was counselling was agreeing that this reflected her personal experience. Often the woman would chime in to say that it sounded as if I had met her husband.

I explained to my clients that, ironically, although they were the ones coming for counselling, they were actually the healthier ones capable of feeling emotions more deeply, caring for others, and making changes. In contrast, the abusers, if they met the criteria for personality disorders, were the unhealthy ones and were unlikely to benefit from counselling.

Precisely because individuals with narcissistic personality disorder are rarely seen by counsellors, the diagnosis is usually based on information from people who have been in close relationships with them over months and years, such as wives and partners.

I would explain to the woman being counselled that while it was vital that she have more accurate knowledge about her partner, she should never share the information about narcissism with the abuser. It is important for a woman in such a situation to realize that there is nothing she can do to change her partner's disordered thinking patterns. I would explain to the woman that the reason the relationship was not working was because any relationship with someone who thinks, feels, and acts like this is unlikely to succeed. I once had a case where a Catholic woman had her marriage annulled when I explained to her bishop about the inability of individuals with personality disorders to fulfil their marriage vows.

After explaining the disorder to the woman and speculating that her abusive partner may have such a disorder, I would then give her homework to do by checking out the description of narcissism at www.narcissisticpersonalitydisorder and ask her to come back and share with me the extent to which she felt that her partner met the criteria described there. Some women have had to do this research secretly at a public library or a friend's house if the abuser shared the computer and could see what sites she had visited. I also stressed to the woman that there are degrees of unhealthiness within personality disorders. If there are only a few traits, then the person with the disorder may be better described as having some narcissistic traits. If, however, her research and our conversations revealed that her partner exhibited almost all the traits most of the time with most people, then he likely fit the diagnostic criteria for a personality disorder. Everyone is unique, and some individuals have characteristics of several of the other personality disorders, such as antisocial personality disorder (especially if he has engaged in illegal behaviour) or dependent personality disorder (if he hands over all the decisions and responsibilities to her). Regardless of the type of personality disorder, it is important for the woman to know that this is a true psychiatric illness for which there is little in the way of treatment. The knowledge that counselling and even medication have little to offer these disordered individuals often enables the woman to understand more fully why her own efforts to change him have been futile.

Let's check in with our fictional Marie again.

᪥

"Well Marie," I said, "what did you discover when you looked up the website about narcissistic personalities?"

"To be honest," she replied, "I was somewhat relieved. I know that some of the things they were describing fit with Steve, but not everything. He does come across as arrogant, but I think it may be that he feels inferior at times and is just trying to put on a show. His dad always treated him badly, and I think sometimes he just doesn't know how to be a good husband or father. I think that his work is more stressful now that he has been promoted. He is still pretty self-centred and critical and hard to live with, but I get glimpses of how he could be when he is kind to Stevie. I think part of the problem is that his mom really spoiled him to make up for his father being so distant, so he is used to having his own needs take priority."

"That is good news Marie," I added. "From what you are telling me, it sounds like Steve has some narcissistic or self-centred traits but not a true narcissistic personality disorder."

"I do understand that even if he has these traits, he should still be treating me better. I hadn't really thought of it as abuse, more like disrespect, but I do want it to change so I can feel better about myself. It was helpful to realize that Steve is mainly the source of the problem, but maybe I am contributing to it by not being very assertive with him. I was really reluctant to admit that I am a victim of emotional abuse, but I can see now that the way that he treats me fits that picture. I remember what you said about how highly sensitive people really need to be in healthy relationships or they can get depressed, and I see now that my feelings of anxiety and depression have been primarily because of how I feel when Steve treats me badly."

One question that women often asked at this stage was "Why didn't I notice some of these things about my partner when we first met?" More commonly, they asked, "Why didn't I make a better choice of partner?"

In response, I would point out that universities should be offering courses in how to choose a healthy partner, but they don't. It is only the most important decision in life, but we don't educate young people on it in any formal way. There is much more education around childbirth, which is limited to a fun-filled nine to twenty-four hours than there is around choosing a life partner. Unfortunately, it is often only when the woman is in the midst of a divorce that the opportunity presents itself to educate her about making a better choice.

I would also explain to the women that many narcissistic men want a woman who is a combination of mother figure and sexual partner. They are on the lookout for a woman who is caring, underassertive puts other people's needs ahead of her own, and generally has few, if any, expressed needs of her own. They certainly don't want a woman whom they perceive as high maintenance, although once married they will accuse the woman of that even if she asks for her very basic human needs, such as kindness and respect, to be met.

Because many Christian woman are "givers" and believe that their role in life is to help other people, they are at risk of being targeted by a narcissist. Giving to others is expected of us as Christians, but in most cases, there is some degree of reciprocity or at least thankfulness. But the narcissist can't do reciprocity or thankfulness. Some women, by their reluctance to ask for their own needs to be met and by their constant striving to meet their partners' needs at the expense of their own, can actually encourage more narcissistic behaviour in their partners.

There is also a gender difference in play here. For the most part, the more that a woman does for another woman, the more that woman will feel obliged to reciprocate. However, in contrast, the more a woman does for a man (even a normal, healthy man), the less he reciprocates, as he assumes that she wouldn't be doing these things for him if she didn't want to. He concludes that because he would not be doing something for her unless he wanted to do it.

If a highly sensitive woman is suffering from low self-esteem, then she may be very vulnerable to a narcissist's initial tactics of wanting to be with her all the time (often to the exclusion of her friends), buying her gifts, and bombarding her with expressions of undying love. Because narcissistic men are primarily interested in the pursuit, they will pull out all the stops to get a woman interested in them and commit to a relationship. A narcissistic man will often tell a woman that no other woman has ever made him feel this way, putting her on a pedestal, which inevitably means he will be disappointed afterward.

The narcissist also will pressure the woman to move more quickly to sexual intimacy than she may be comfortable with. This presents another problem, especially for Christian women who have been taught that sexual intimacy is reserved for marriage. If she has been persuaded to engage in sexual intercourse in the early stages of the relationship, then she will be at risk for persuading herself that she loves the man. She does this to maintain a positive view of herself, and the situation; however, this means that she may ignore warning signs that going forward with the relationship is not a good option. Many narcissistic men can be skillful lovers if it gets them what they want. And a sexually naive woman may mistake her partner's intense sexual pursuit as proof of his love for her.

Many women describe the courtship period with phrases like "swept off my feet" and "I never met a man who was so interested in me before." During this time prior to marriage, the man does his best to stay up at "normal" and does not show her his darker side.

Depending on several factors, this span, known as the "honeymoon period," can last weeks or months. Often the woman does not notice the subtle changes in her partner's behaviour until after the birth of their first child. At that point, the woman naturally gives most of her attention to the new baby, but narcissistic males resent that and will become more demanding or will look elsewhere to get their needs met. One woman told me that her husband changed on their wedding night into a raging, angry abuser. However, most are okay as long as they feel they have their partners' undivided attention, which is usually the case until children arrive.

Many brilliant sensitive women have been taken in by narcissists because narcissists are so skilled at manipulating people. Because of a narcissistic man's initial charming behaviour, a woman who enters a relationship with him believes that this initial "self" is who he truly is and that when the critical, abusive side begins to show up, it is due to "work stress," some other external problem, or her own failings. This false belief on her part keeps her connected and optimistic, remembering how her partner used to be and hoping to recapture that original relationship. It also solidifies her belief that it must be her fault. She needs to understand that the person she saw initially during the "honeymoon" phase was fake and that she is now seeing his true self, which unfortunately may be very disordered.

Now let's check in with Stella, who, like Marie, was also asked to explore personality disorders.

"Stella, I am interested to know what you discovered when you checked out the website for your husband" I said.

Stella opened her purse and took out several sheets of paper.

"There was so much I found out that I wanted to write it all down so I could tell you," she said. "First of all, Alex thinks he is the most important person in his workplace. He is a lower-level manager, but he is always talking about how he could improve things if he just got the chance. He is always going on about how his boss never listens to his ideas and is always trying to cut him off, but I think his boss just gets tired of him being such a know-it-all and giving all this unwanted advice.

"He is always exaggerating what he does at work. I overheard him telling our son that he was going to be up for a big promotion any day now because he works so hard. Meanwhile, my friend Betty works in the same office, and she says he sits around all day telling everyone how to do their jobs and not doing his own. Anything that he doesn't like to do at work he just pawns off on his staff and then passes it off as his own work. I am sure they all hate him, but he is really good at praising the big boss, who thinks he is wonderful, and so they are afraid to say anything against him.

"Ever since we got married, Alex always seemed to need a lot of attention and admiration. If I forget to thank him for doing the dishes, he gets really annoyed or sulks, saying he deserves thanks for all the things he does for me. Yeah right! He only does things if I ask him several times, and lately it is just easier for me to do things myself because he makes such a big deal out of doing even the smallest chore.

"He is always monopolizing the conversation. If I try to tell him about my day, or even some problem I might be having he will scoff at me and say that he had things much worse.

"It is like he can't stand it if someone else has done something better than him, so he denigrates what other people do.

"I feel bad for our son because Alex is always ragging on him about trying out for the varsity football team. Kris just wants to join the debate club and play chess, but Alex tells him that is for sissies and makes fun of him. Alex did play football in university but then injured his knee and was out for the rest of the season, but to hear him tell it, he was the best thing that ever happened to the team, and without him they wouldn't have made the playoffs. Actually, I learned later that it was after he was benched that they started to do better, because before that he was always creating conflict within the team.

"Alex is also really envious of our neighbours. They have good jobs and work hard, and they have a lovely house and yard and a new car every few years, but Alex can't stop badmouthing them to me. He keeps saying that the husband must be working under the table to afford the things they have, but that's not true. I try to point out to Alex that maybe they don't spend money on alcohol and gaming like he does, we could have a better car too. He seems to feel like he deserves all these privileges in life but doesn't see that he should work hard to achieve them. He blames me when we can't afford something.

"He is also a bottomless pit. If I do something nice for him, he will be happy for a moment but an hour later will tear a strip off me for not knowing where he put his keys.

"The other thing he does is always compare me to the women at work, all of whom are younger and single. He tells me that they are all fawning over him and how he has to fend them off. He tells me that maybe if I started dressing better, he might want to have sex with me. I know he looks at pornography, because he tells me I should do what the women in the porno videos do.

"He never tells me what his actual salary is, because he is very secretive about finances. He says I should be paying half of all the household expenses, but I know my salary is likely less than half of what he makes. He will let the bills pile up until I get so frustrated that I end up asking my boss for an advance on my pay. Then he just gloats and says he feels tired and takes a week off to go golfing."

"Stella," I said, "it sounds like your husband has most of the traits of narcissistic personality disorder, and that is a really serious problem because these individuals are not very receptive to change."

"I know," Stella added. "I have been trying to figure out how to handle it, but it just seems to get worse as the years go by. Now he is talking of quitting his job and retiring early, but I don't see how we can manage financially if that happens.

"I guess I have just been really stupid not realizing how bad our marriage has been. I just kept hoping that I could figure out how to make it better, but everything I have tried has failed."

⁂

Many times, once a woman begins to recognize the depth of her partner's disorder, she will berate herself for being "stupid" for not noticing the red flags.

With women such as Stella, I would reframe stupidity as excessive hopefulness in that they keep hoping despite all odds that they will be able to fix the situation or that their partners will eventually see the light. If the woman holds on to the view that she is stupid, then it is harder for her to imagine that she can change things; however, if she can see that it was really her hopefulness that led her astray, then she can take steps to make changes.

I reminded Stella that we often get into trouble because of our strengths, not because of our weaknesses. The very thing that makes a woman excellent at her job (e.g., wonderful patience with teaching young children) can be a handicap if she applies that same patience and hopefulness to someone who is not motivated or able to change his behaviour.

All people want to believe that they can change situations by their own efforts, prayers, or tactics.

I wanted Stella to understand that there was absolutely nothing she could have done differently that would have changed the outcome. If trained counsellors working for years cannot change individuals with personality disorders, then it was unrealistic for her to assume that she could change her partner. She had to let go of this false hope, but doing so can be sad, as that had kept her connected and trying to improve the relationship with her own efforts.

For Christian women who have been praying that God will change their partners, I remind them that God requires the person himself or herself to want to make changes. God does not change us against our will. I remind such women that because they are basically healthy people, and only healthy people can change, we need to focus on what they themselves can change. When a woman accepts that she cannot change her partner, she often goes through a grieving process. She is grieving the loss of the hope that has sustained her all these years. We can then focus on acknowledging the depth of the abuse and grieving the loss of the love that she has been hoping for.

*Have her write and read a
confidential letter to her abuser.*

One method I found that helps women to move forward in the grieving process is adapted from Susan Forward's book *Toxic Parents.* She recommends writing letters to the abusive person and then sitting down with the abuser and reading it to him or her.

For many survivors of abuse, writing such a letter is like having their day in court. Even though victim impact statements in court don't change the outcome of the trial, they do allow the victim to tell others about the depth of their suffering.

I would ask the woman to write a letter to her abuser stating all the sad and angry things that she was never able to tell him directly out of fear of reprisal, but I would have her read it only to me and possibly a trusted friend. Again, this is not to be shared with the abuser, as doing so would put her at risk of more abuse.

Now let's return to our fictional Marie.

♔

"Have you written your letter to Steve yet?" I asked Marie.

"Yes," she replied. "It took me about a week before I felt up to doing it, but knowing that I had an appointment with you today, I decided to write it last night."

"I know it was hard for you," I replied, "but I am very proud of you for having the courage to do it. Can you read it to me out loud now?"

Marie took a sheaf of papers out of her purse and started to read.

"'Dear Steve, my counsellor says that writing this letter will help me deal with my anger and frustration with you, so here goes.

"'I guess I am most angry because I feel betrayed and sad because you turned out to be so different than what I thought you were like when we first met.

"'You used to tell me how much you loved me and how you couldn't wait to see me each day. You would even send me a poem or a funny cartoon that you thought I might like.

"'You always used to bring me flowers every Saturday, and I am ashamed to admit that I didn't really want flowers. I just wanted you to listen to me tell you about my day.

"'You never asked me my opinion about anything. You just kept spouting off your own and generally criticizing everyone at your work or in the government. If I tried to interject something, you would just talk over me as if what I had to say wasn't really important. You loved to remind me that your family was better off than mine and that your mom was a Julia Child–trained cook whereas my mom is not a great cook. I know I wasn't as sophisticated when we first met and you liked to buy me clothes that were more stylish. But even when I became more sophisticated, it was as if you always saw me as some country bumpkin that needed educating. I hated how you always bragged to our friends about your job but then complained to me. I know you liked to be the centre of attention, but sometimes it was really embarrassing for me, as I could tell our friends were inwardly rolling their eyes. You always had to play the role of the rich guy, paying for everyone's meals at a restaurant, but then you wouldn't give me a budget for groceries. I hated having to always ask you for money, and you would question anything I bought for the baby, meanwhile splurging on new golf clubs, gym memberships, or weekend trips away. I hated how you always talked about how some other guys' wives were better than me—how they dressed better or cooked better meals. And it was hard for me when you kept going over to your mom's place so much.

"'It was hard for me in the church, too, because you were always so charming to everyone else, and several women told me how lucky they thought I was to be married to you.

"'You could never understand that I just wanted you to respect me and treat me with kindness and caring. Even when you did something wrong, you never apologized. Somehow you managed to blame every problem on me. If I tried to get you to see my side of the story by the time we finished talking, you would have convinced me that I was the one with the problem.

"'I also hated how you were so secretive about what you were doing on the computer, always shutting it down when I came into the room. At first, I made a joke of it, asking if you were working for a spy agency, but you just got offended. In fact, you seemed to be offended at even the tiniest criticism of your behaviour. Even if I asked for something small, you would make it seem like I was this unreasonable person who was making your life difficult by being so demanding. I was really hurt when you were not with me at Stevie's birth, and I didn't really believe that your boss wouldn't have given you the time off. Maybe you were worried about being fired. You never even went to any of the prenatal classes with me or bothered to read the books.

"'You talk about Stevie to other people a lot—especially if he has done something advanced for his age. But you don't seem to actually want to spend time with him. I think he understands that sometimes and starts to cry for me to come and play with him instead.

"'It would be nice if you could be more encouraging about my interior decorating career. You always put it down and tell me I am wasting my time. But I really want a little bit of my own money so that I don't always have to come to you for money. For someone who doesn't want to spend much time with me any more (except for sex, that is) you seem to always want to know where I am going or who I am with. By the way sex, would be much better if you would read that book by John Gray that I put on your beside table—*Mars and Venus in the Bedroom*. It talks about how many men just don't know how to please their wives, and I was impressed with how much it described our relationship. But I see it is covered up with golf magazines. I guess you figure you know all there is to know about pleasing me and no book can teach you anything. I would like to have a better sex life, not one where I have to pretend I am enjoying it, because if I don't, then you get really annoyed. Maybe you are getting your needs met on the Internet these days and don't need the real thing so much any more.

"'I am so disappointed that we can't have an honest discussion about our problems without you taking offence and stomping off. You always revert to how you are paying the bills and how I should be happy with that, but I would really like to have a true partner that I can trust and that is supportive of me when I feel down.

"'I guess I haven't realized how many things I am angry about until I started writing this letter. I know that my counsellor has been talking to me about how you have narcissistic traits, and I guess this is what she meant. It helps to know that most of the time you are not doing this to me on purpose, but just because I understand that doesn't make you any easier to live with. I really hoped that we could go to a marriage counsellor, but you have such a negative attitude about them that I just gave up. I just hope I can find a way to deal with how unhappy I am in this marriage. Yours truly, Marie.'"

⚜

Now let's see how Stella managed with the same homework exercise.

⚜

"Hello, Stella," I said at my next session with her. "Have you had a chance to write your letter to Alex yet?"

"Yes," she replied. "I went over to my girlfriend's house on the weekend for a break, and I wrote it there, on her computer.

She knows how hard it has been for me with Alex, and I know I can go over there anytime I need a break. Here goes.

"'Alex, this letter has been a long time coming. Right from the beginning, I thought that something was a little off. I came close to calling off the wedding, but my mom said I couldn't because they had invited so many people and didn't want to be embarrassed.

"'Our honeymoon was awful because I didn't really know much about sex and you were really rough and didn't make any effort to please me. From that point on, I really dreaded having sex, but I knew you would be really angry, so I pretended it was great.

"'I knew that you were having affairs right after our first child was born because I came across your phone and found all these texts to a woman that I didn't recognize, and they were really intimate. I didn't want to tell you, because I knew you would accuse me of snooping, and I hoped that it would end on its own.

"'I should have seen some red flags, like you having so many different jobs over the years, but I guess I just believed you when you said that your bosses just didn't appreciate how smart you were. It was hard because we would just get settled in one place and then you would announce that we were going to move again. You always made a big deal about me getting back to work soon after the kids were born. I was really hoping to stay home with them for a few years, but with you always changing jobs, it was clear we needed a steady income.

"'I hated how you always controlled the money, even if it was my money that I was bringing in. You would nickel-and-dime me over clothes for the kids, meanwhile having to have a big-screen

TV and all the latest electronic gadgets. Money was always a big deal for you, but you never really worked hard to make it.

"'It upset me that you were always so involved in the church that you never had time for the kids. You were always going to some meeting or other or organizing something for the pastor, but meanwhile I really could have used the help at home. You always handed over to me anything that you didn't want to do or be involved with. Sometimes I felt pretty much like a single parent, as everything to do with the kids was always up to me—even driving them to band practice in the evenings. Plus, you never offered to help cook or clean or even do the grocery shopping, so life was really busy, especially when the kids were younger. Kris was a pretty easy child, but Emily was a challenge, and I could have really used your help with managing them.

"'It was hard to hear the people at the church raving about what a great help you were to everybody there, especially the single women. You were always ready to help move somebody or deliver groceries if someone was sick, but you always managed to get people to notice what you were doing. You probably thought I didn't notice how you flirted with all the other women, but I did, and it was hard to take. But I didn't want to let on that it bothered me, so I just laughed it off and said, "That's just Alex."

"'It did become a problem when you started spending so much time with the church secretary. You claimed that you were just helping her with office work, but it seemed to happen more when the pastor was away. She always seemed a little awkward around me, and I suspected that you were having an affair. At one point, my friend asked me about it, but I just brushed it off because I didn't want to face the fact that you were unfaithful again.

"'I was always puzzled by how you could be so charming to people outside the family and so harsh and rude with the kids and me. I tried talking to our pastor, but he thought you were wonderful, so he just patted my hand and said I was imagining things.

"'I feel so beaten down and discouraged because everything I tried to do to make things work has failed. Now I don't really have the energy to deal with you, so we just coexist, rarely talking except when you want something from me or when you criticize me.

"'I guess at this stage I feel like I don't want to waste the rest of my life living this sham, but I don't know if I can muster the strength to leave. I have been hanging on until both the kids finish high school, which they do this year. I hope I can do something to feel better about myself, but I am not sure what my options are. Stella.'"

When a woman would read her letter out loud to me, I would have the opportunity to offer her comfort and encouragement for her bravery in tolerating the abuse over the months and years. Often both of us would be in tears in that session. I would then tell the woman that I was so sorry that she had to suffer not being loved, and I would remind her that God loves her and that He was sad to know how badly she had been treated. It was really important that the woman received this apology from me, as it acknowledged the extent of her suffering and allowed her to process her grief.

If she was a highly sensitive person (like Marie), then I would remind her that being a in a relationship with someone with narcissist traits is a terrible combination, as the narcissist represents the extreme of insensitivity. I would remind her again that the impact of living with someone like her abuser is much more impactful than it would be if she were not a highly sensitive person. It is vital that a woman in such a situation understand how dangerous the situation is to her own mental and emotional health. Highly sensitive women are generally more focused on the needs of others and need to start looking at meeting their own emotional needs.

If the woman I was counselling was not a highly sensitive person (like Stella), then I might commend her for her fortitude in hanging in so long in an abusive relationship. But I would also remind her that just because she may not find it as difficult as someone with a more sensitive temperament doesn't mean that it is okay to be treated badly. If her children had watched the unhealthy dynamics, they may be desensitized to abuse and at risk for making unhealthy choices themselves. Even if a woman in an abusive situation is willing to put up with abuse, it is important that she assess the impact that may have on her children. Normalizing abuse in the context of family relationships can be a precursor to the children being at risk for choosing an abusive partner themselves or being abusive to a future partner.

The process of truly understanding that she cannot change the situation and thus giving up hope means that the woman can also let go of the guilt that she has been carrying that has kept her tied to the abuser. When the woman finally accepts that he is not going to change, she can then focus on herself and her own emotional needs. I had a cartoon in my office that showed an interchange between a man and a woman. The woman was saying to the man, "Remember all those years I used to say ... 'It's not you ... it's me.' Well, apparently, it's not me ... it's you!"

Recognizing that the man is not going to be capable of change is poignant; it is both sad and also freeing because the woman can then stop blaming herself for all the relationship problems.

Once a woman has a clearer picture of her partner and his personality problems, she needs to examine whether there are other problematic relationships in her life.

Evaluate her relationship with her
parents and write her letters to them.

This next step in the guide involves exploring the woman's relationship with her own parents (who may or may not still be living), as that is often a template for her future relationships.

Because delving into childhood memories can be scary for some women, I would often tell clients the story of a dream that one of my clients shared with me. This woman told me that in her dream she was in her kitchen, having tea with a friend who had come over for a visit. Initially they were just chatting normally, but then she became nervous because she knew that any minute her friend would ask to see the rest of her house. She realized that she had never seen the upstairs of her own house, but in the dream, she was embarrassed to say so. As she predicted, her friend asked to see the rest of the house. In the dream, she started up the stairs with the friend trailing behind her. When she got to the top of the stairs, there was a long, dark hallway with a door at the end. She was still fearful, but she continued down the hallway and put her hand out to open the door. When she opened the door, she discovered that the room was filled with light and beautiful plants and soft music. She felt an overwhelming sense of peace and joy.

She told me that she knew that her dream represented her journey with me in confronting the dark passages of her life which held her sadness and pain. But she also knew that if she persisted, she would experience a wonderful freedom and peace at the end. She shared with me that she believed that God had given her this dream to encourage her to have faith that she would be able to face the difficult work ahead and that the outcome would be worth it.

Oftentimes in the sessions, there would be a natural segue from discussing her partner to sharing about her parents. Sometimes when the woman was researching on websites to find information about her partner's behaviour, she would come back and tell me that a site also described her father or mother. Making these connections was a very important step. I helped her see how parents who conditioned her to believe that she was to meet their needs and "make them happy" positioned her to be chosen by a partner who wanted the same thing.

Many women described themselves as "people pleasers." These women were often brainwashed to believe that if they didn't meet their parents' needs, they were bad or selfish, and they carried that legacy into adulthood.

I would sometimes joke with such a woman that if we were both on a sinking ship, I would want her by my side, as she would likely hand me her life jacket.

If the woman and I discovered that one or both of her parents had a personality disorder, then I would ask her to write letters to them as well. But instead of sharing the letters with her parents, I would ask her to read those letters only to me, just as with her letter to her abusive partner. As I listened to her, I had the opportunity to be a caring, loving support to her, and many times I was moved to tears as I listened to her story.

Even if the parent is dead, this is a helpful exercise. One woman said to me, "My father has been dead ten years, but he still lives with me." Interestingly, with one woman I neglected to mention that she should not read the letters to her parents. She wrote her letters, sat her parents down, and read the letters to them. In that particular case, fortunately there was a good outcome; but in most cases, that would not be the situation. Often even if the women tried to tell their parents the truth of their childhoods, the parents would likely deny it or block out that it happened. We all want to hold relatively positive views of ourselves as parents, and so even normal parents block out information that contradicts that view. Some women who have tried to speak the truth about their childhoods to parents have been doubly abused when the parents have denied it and attacked the women for what they labelled as "lies."

At this point, I would spend time listening to the woman tell me more about her experiences with her parents and again offer support and encouragement as she started to recognize similarities between them and her abusive husband. I would often recommend that she read one of the excellent books about disordered parents. In Susan Forward's classic book *Toxic Parents*, the author describes a variety of different types of disordered parents, including more subtle ones, such as the inadequate parent who hands over to a child an excessive amount of responsibility. Usually, the woman could identify with one or more of the examples in the book, and reading about other difficult parents would help her to understand that she was not the only one struggling with these issues. If it was the woman's mother who demonstrated narcissistic traits, I might suggest that she read *Will I Ever Be Good Enough* by Karyl McBride, which specifically addresses narcissistic mothers. After reading more about disordered parents, we would discuss the extent to which her parents resembled the case histories in the books.

I would also remind the woman that disordered parents, like her partner, were incapable of giving her the love and respect that she deserved. Many times, when reading her letters to me, the woman would begin to understand how wrong it was that she was not loved and, looking back on her childhood, would begin to see herself in a different light. Part of this process was also for her to experience me as a caring, comforting parental figure to replace what she didn't have growing up. I would share with her how much God loves her even though her parents may not have been capable of that love. Psalm 27:10 (MSG) says, "My father and mother walked out and left me but God took me in." Even in Biblical times, there were individuals whose parents couldn't give them the love they needed, but God filled that void and would do so with her. I would remind her that God has promised to be a Father to the Fatherless and that He keeps His promise to us even when others let us down. God says, "I'll never let you down, never walk off and leave you" (Hebrews 13:5 MSG).

Disordered parents range from mild to severe, and some are purposely abusive, whereas others are abusive simply because they cannot see beyond their own needs. Once the woman had a clearer picture of her parents' limitations, she could usually see them as damaged and disabled by their mental disorder rather than always purposely abusive.

I would sometimes suggest to her that if she had a parent who was in a wheelchair, she would not expect that parent to be able to do certain things to meet her needs. Since her parents were emotionally and psychologically disabled, she could not expect that they would be able to truly love her and meet her basic needs for safety and security. Many disordered parents have times when they pop up to normalcy and function in a fairly healthy way. Ironically, this often makes things worse for their daughters, as they then may be convinced that their parents should be able to remain in this higher-functioning state. This belief fuels more false hopes and sets such women up for more disappointments.

When a woman is able to see her parents in a more realistic light, she may well be relieved to understand why they were unable to love her. This corrected version of reality is certainly preferable to her previous conclusion, which was that they didn't love her because she was unlovable.

Having disordered parents is a terrible legacy for anyone and typically engenders two polar opposite responses in a child. For some children (often males), the knowledge that a parent really doesn't love them is so painful that they block it out and determine that they will meet their own needs going forward. Such individuals can end up being narcissistic out of a sense of compensation for not having their needs met. It is as if they are saying, "My parents didn't care about my needs, so I am going to make sure that I get my needs met myself."

In contrast, for some other children (often females), having a narcissistic parent means that they will try very hard to meet the parent's needs in the hope that the parent will love them. This is the victim role, but it is also the hopeful role and one that society rewards in women because then they focus all their attention on the other person. Employers and friends praise these women because they put the needs of their bosses, colleagues, or friends ahead of their own.

The following is another conversation with our fictional Marie.

"So, Marie," I said, "Did you get your letters written to your parents this week?"

"Yes I did," she replied. "Actually, it was ironic, because I knew Steve was feeling guilty about something because he asked me if I needed something (which he never does). So I told him that I needed a few hours to work on a project and that it would be helpful if he could look after Stevie during that time. He agreed, so it gave me time to write my letters. The first one is to my dad.

"'Dear Dad, I know you would be so hurt and angry to know that I am writing this letter about you, because you always told me how lucky I was to have a good father like you. When I was a little girl, I always looked up to you because you seemed larger than life. When you entered a room, you controlled the room. Everyone would stop talking and wait to see what kind of mood you were in before we could relax. You were really hard on my brother, John, because you wanted him to follow you into business, but he just wanted to be an artist. You bullied him and told him you would not support him going to art school, but he persisted, and I was proud of him for standing up to you.

"'You never really paid much attention to me, probably because I was shy and I tried to blend into the woodwork so you wouldn't notice me. My sister, Bonnie, was just the opposite, and you and she were always arguing. You were always criticizing everything she did, and eventually she just gave up and moved in with her boyfriend. You stopped talking about her then, and it really scared me that you could be so cold toward your own child. I decided I would try hard to make you happy so you would never do that to me. I knew that you always liked things to be organized, and Mom wasn't very good at that, so I would go around and pick up after you and put things away so it would look neat and tidy.

"'I was always afraid of your moods. Sometimes you could be so jolly and fun and wanted to play card games, but other times you would just sit in your armchair and scowl at no one in particular. At those times, your breath smelled funny, and I began to understand that you had been drinking. Everybody was nervous when you drank. Mom just went to bed saying she had a headache, so it was just us kids with you then. I tried to help you get up the stairs to bed, and sometimes you would tell me that I was the only one who cared about you. I guess I felt proud that you were saying that to me. Certainly, John and Bonnie made themselves scarce as well. But sometimes even if I did what you wanted, you still yelled at me, and I never knew if you were going to be happy with me or not. I just always wanted to please you, and I tried my best. Sometimes it worked, and sometimes no matter what I did, you were upset.

"'Dad, it seemed like you placed a big load on me to be your support, especially when you had been drinking, and I think that deep down I resented it but also felt I had a special role to play in the family—that of peacemaker. I really resent that you don't want to spend much time with Stevie, as he is your only grandson, and also that you won't let Mom come over to be a help to me. But I guess I know by now that if it isn't something you want to do, it just doesn't happen. I do appreciate that you were always a hard worker and we never went without when we were kids. I just wish you could have spent more time connecting with us rather than just lecturing about what we should and shouldn't do.

"'Your daughter, Marie.'

"'Dear Mom,

I think the word that comes to my mind when I am writing this letter to you is "weak." You always seemed to be on the verge of a nervous breakdown, and I never felt that I could share any of my concerns with you or even talk to you about Dad. Your family was British, and the stiff-upper-lip mentality meant that people didn't talk about their feelings. You must have known when you took to your bed that you were leaving me to deal with Dad, but it seems like you didn't care enough to try to protect me. Mothers are supposed to protect their children, but I always felt I had to protect you because you were so frail. I couldn't believe that you had a job before you met Dad, because you let him make all the decisions. He tells you what to cook and how to dress and makes sure that you account for every dollar he gives you to spend. You never criticize him, even when he spends money on alcohol, and you didn't even stand up for Bonnie when he bullied her. I can see why she wanted to move out. You always tell me to just be quiet and do what Dad wants so he won't get upset. I know Bonnie's strategy of confronting him didn't work. He just seems so self-centered. He is only concerned about his own needs, and he never does anything nice for you. I feel sorry for you, but I am also annoyed that you are so passive and don't stand up for yourself. You even let Dad convince you not to go back to work. You were a talented dress designer before you got married, and I would think you would have wanted to continue that, but apparently Dad didn't want people thinking that he couldn't support his own family, so he didn't allow you to go back to your job.

"'I feel sad sometimes when I get a brief glimpse of who you were before you met Dad. That summer when your sister visited, I got to listen to the two of you talking about old times. You were so animated and funny, and I remember thinking that it was so sad that the person you could have been just got beaten down so that you just went along with whatever Dad wanted. I wanted to be able to tell you my problems, but at some level I knew that you wanted to believe that I would always be the strong one even for you. You could hardly look after yourself, let alone children. I guess that is why I decided to learn to cook when I was a teenager, because sometimes you wouldn't have the energy to prepare supper. I know that you believed in God and even attended a woman's Bible study, but it didn't seem to translate into you having the strength to confront Dad. I guess part of my anger is that I didn't want a mother that I had to feel sorry for; I wanted a mother who would be there for me emotionally, and you just could never do that. I don't know what will happen in the future now that you are a grandmother to baby Stevie, but I hope you can somehow learn to be stronger for him and me.

"'Love, Marie.'"

"So Marie," I said, "it sounds like your dad has some narcissistic traits just like Steve."

"Yes," Marie replied. "I was noticing that when I was researching about narcissistic personalities. I kept thinking that some of it described my dad. It is funny that I am only starting to see the resemblance between him and Steve now.

"I was also thinking that in some ways I have been tolerating Steve's behaviour the way my mom tolerated my dad's. I always thought I was stronger than my mom, but now I realize that I have to work on being more assertive myself. Maybe if I were stronger, Steve wouldn't be the way he is."

Often at this stage, the woman I was seeing would report that she was now starting to feel the previously suppressed anger toward her disordered parents. I would validate her feelings of anger and tell her that it was understandable and normal to feel that way. I would remind the woman that she could hand over to God the eventual punishment of her abusers. The Bible verse "Vengeance is mine says the Lord, I will repay" (Romans 12:9 NIV) is a reminder that we don't need to take punishment into our own hands. When a woman tells me that she cannot forgive her parents, I explain that forgiveness does not mean forgetting what the abuser has done and will continue to do unless a different strategy is employed. Forgiveness also does not mean that a woman continues to allow her partner or her parent to treat her disrespectfully. I would remind each woman I counselled that she was a beloved child of God, worthy of kindness and respect even if her partner (or parents) did not show her that. I would also explain that in extending forgiveness to her abusers, she could eventually let go of her unhealthy emotions which were preventing her from healing. I would tell her that after we looked at her other relationships, I would help her learn some assertive strategies to deal with the anger and fear that she felt toward the abusive people in her life.

At that point, I would also take time to explore whether the woman could recall God providing her with any "surrogate" parents, teachers, or coaches who helped her along her journey and may have compensated for the lack of support from her parents. Remembering these individuals gives a woman a perspective on how God met her needs in the past and will continue to do so in the future.

The following is another conversation with our fictional Marie.

☙

"So Marie," I asked, "when you think back, were there any adults in your life that stepped in and made you feel like they really cared about you?"

Marie thought for a moment and then replied. "Yes, now that you mention it, there was this sweet little lady who lived by herself a few doors down from our house. Often when I was walking home from school, she would be out in her front yard, tending to her roses, and she would call me over to ask how I was doing. Usually she would invite me to come in and have a cookie and hot chocolate with her. She wasn't like a lot of elderly people who just want to talk about their illnesses. She seemed genuinely interested in me. Sometimes I would show her my homework and she would help me with it, or she would find a book that had the answers. She had this bookcase with all twenty-four volumes of the Encyclopaedia Britannica in it, and when we came across a problem, she would go and pull down those big heavy books and read to me. This was before my family got a computer and could find things on the Internet, so it was great to have that help. She said that she bought the books one per month when she was working as a teacher, and the company even sold her the special bookcase that fit them all.

"Mrs. Christy was her name, and her children all lived far away, so I think she was lonely. Sometimes if I was looking down in the dumps, she would tell me stories from her childhood of growing up on a farm and having trouble making ends meet. My problems seemed small compared to hers, but she always told me that you can't ever compare your pain to someone else's. Besides, she talked a lot about God and how she was blessed to still be healthy and able to live on her own. At Christmas I didn't have much money, but I gave her a lovely embroidered handkerchief in a pale purple box, and she said it was so beautiful that she used it as a placemat for her vase of flowers. She loved flowers, and she always smelled nice because she dusted herself with lavender powder each day. She died a few years ago, but I always think of her when I smell lavender. I guess you are right; God did send Mrs. Christy to be there with me when I needed someone to talk to. It is true that she made up for what I missed with my mom. Thanks for reminding me of that."

♔

Now let's see how Stella made out with her letters to her parents.

♔

"Well, Stella," I asked. "Did you get a chance to write the letters to your mom and dad?

"Yes, I did," she replied, "and even though I cried while I was writing, I felt better by the end. I don't think I really realized how much I had bottled up and never dealt with before."

Let's hear you read it," I said.

"'Dear Mom,

I guess I always thought you were an okay mom, but the more I read about unhealthy personalities, the more I realize that I was wrong about you. You always had to have the best of everything. Your clothes, makeup, and hair were always done to perfection. Poor Dad was always trying to buy you what you wanted and sometimes going into debt to do it.

"'Any time I brought home a boyfriend, you would insist on sitting with us and dominating the conversation. You could be very charming with men, and sometimes my boyfriends would tell me how lucky I was to have a mother like you.

"'You hounded me about my grades even though I was always in the top 10 per cent of my class. If I got a B+, you would ask why I didn't get an A.

"'Sometimes I think you had no boundaries, because you would sneak into my room when I was at school and read my diary. I learned to lock it up and wear the key around my neck.

"'Dealing with your moods was the hardest. I could never predict if you were going to be pleasant and charming or really rude and harsh. It was like walking on eggshells for both Dad and me. Dad was a sweet man, but he just did whatever you wanted to keep the peace. I sometimes wondered why he would take so long to get groceries, but I suspected it was because he got a break from your nagging.

"'You never asked me about my feelings or hopes for the future. It was as if you didn't think I would amount to anything. I really struggled with low self-esteem, and so when I met Alex, he was the first man to really pay attention to me. You thought he was great, and you and he got along so well that I thought he must be okay. Dad was not so impressed with Alex, and he told me he thought I could do better, but you made me think I had better grab Alex before he could get away, because nobody else would want me.

"'Even now that you are older, you are still so demanding of me and critical that I jump when the phone rings and I know it is likely going to be you.

"'I hadn't realized until I started writing this letter how much my stress and anxiety with Alex is made worse by you. You always take his side when I try to tell you how he treats me, and you tell me I should be really thankful for such a great husband. I know that he hits you up for money and you give it to him for some of his "trips away," saying he needs a break because his job is so stressful. He is always so flattering to you, telling you that you look half your age and how if you were younger you would have been the one he married. You never seem to grasp how insulting all that is to me.

"'You are still really demanding of me, and sometimes it is all I can do to keep from screaming at you to give me a break. But you have that way of looking at me with such disgust that I am afraid of what you might do if I stood up to you. I really don't think that you need me to do your laundry when you have a washer and dryer in your condo, but you always tell me that I do a better job. I get sucked in when you praise me, but those times are few and far between. My friends say I am just being used, but I can't seem to say no to you, especially when you tell me how sick you are and how you probably won't make it until Christmas. I really want to honour you like the Bible says, but it would be nice to have a thank-you now and then.

"'Poor Dad. Now that he is dead, I understand what he had to put up with. But he never complained. I guess I am more like Dad, and I want to be a caring daughter, but it just feels hard never to be appreciated for anything I do. Maybe my counsellor can help me figure out how to handle things with you, too. Love, Stella.'

"'Dear Dad,

"'This will be a shorter letter because you weren't around very much when I was growing up. You travelled a lot with your job as a salesman and were often out of town. When you did get back, you were often so tired that you just ended up sleeping a lot. You were never cross or angry with us, but looking back, I wonder if maybe you were depressed. Mom was always so critical of you, just like she was of me, so I thought we might bond because of that. But you never stood up to her, and you always told me just to do what she asked so she would be happy. I know it was always better when she was in a good mood, but I just wanted you to take my side sometimes. You and Mom seemed to have fun when other people were around, but when it was just the two of you, it was often deathly silent.

"'I wanted you to be strong and tell Mom when she was shouting and screaming that it wasn't okay, but you just sat there and waited until she ran out of steam. I guess that is where I learned to just tolerate her behaviour. Now I realize that it was actually abusive and you never did anything about it. I know Mom always made a big deal about how she married beneath her and had all these different marriage proposals. But she thought you looked so handsome in your navy uniform that she chose you. I guess you must have had fun when you and Mom were younger, but after we kids arrived and Mom didn't want to go back to work, things were tough. I guess you thought that if you just bought her all the things she wanted, she would be happy, but she never was.

"'Anyway, Dad, I know you did the best you could, and I am thankful for those times that you came in to tell me goodnight and sat on my bed and listened to me tell you about school. Even though you didn't say it, I know that you loved me, and that was a really important gift. I just wish you could have been stronger with Mom and stood up to her when she treated me badly. But I know you didn't want to make waves.

"'I wish you were still here, because now it's up to me to look after her. But I bet you are glad in some ways that you are finally at rest with God. Love, Stella.'"

"What did you conclude after writing these letters and researching the websites?" I asked Stella.

"I think I was most surprised to discover that my mom really fit most of the criteria for narcissistic personality disorder," she replied. "I knew she wasn't a great mother, but I didn't really fully understand that because she was so wrapped up in herself, she really couldn't love me or validate me the way that I wanted. I knew my dad loved me, but he was always so passive with her, and I guess I just figured out that was the way to handle someone like my mom. I really thought when I married Alex that he would love me and make up for what I didn't get from my parents. I didn't really need a lot, as I am pretty independent, but I guess in a way that prevented me from seeing the reality that I married someone who resembled my mom. For much of my life, I tried to minimize my contact with my mom. I was always busy with my work. But since my dad died, I have had to have more contact with her, and I have started to notice more things about her that really bother me."

To my surprise, an informal chart survey I conducted a number of years ago found that about 74 per cent of women who were married to a man with a narcissistic personality also had one or both parents with a disordered personality. This is why it is very important to explore family-of-origin issues with abused women. There is another very interesting reason why we need to tackle the original family of an abused woman. If the woman had a narcissistic parent, she would be at risk for not recognizing unhealthy personality traits in the early stages of her relationship with her partner. She may have tolerated some of the uncomfortable interactions with her partner and even viewed them as normal, as they would have been familiar because of her childhood experiences. The woman may also have believed (consciously or unconsciously) that she could use the same strategies with her spouse that she used with a parent, only to discover later on that these strategies resulted in failure.

*Evaluate the healthiness of her
church, friends and employer.*

Years ago, I read a book entitled *The Subtle Power of Spiritual Abuse*
by David W. Johnson and Jeff VanVonderen. It highlighted
some of the abuse that sometimes inadvertently or even directly is
perpetrated on both women and men in the church. If a woman
in an abusive situation is a Christian and attends a church, it is
important to spend time looking at what the response has been
from the church to her abuse. For many Christians, talking about
abuse is not encouraged. They may feel they have to perpetuate
a myth that with faith in God, any obstacles can be overcome.
For the most part, women in a church setting are very reluctant
to discuss being abused, and this is especially true if their abusive
partners are elders or even pastors. They believe, often correctly,
that they will not be believed because other people's experiences
of their partners can be so different.

If the abused woman had been pressured to keep quiet about the abuse and forgive the abuser, then discussing forgiveness with her again in more detail was required. I would remind the woman that at some point her partner would be judged before God and that if she enabled the abuse to continue by not being assertive, then she was ultimately not helping her partner prepare to stand before God's judgement.

A woman in an abusive situation needs to evaluate whether her church is a source of support and encouragement or whether she is finding herself blamed or ignored if she talks about the abuse. Depending on the answers, the woman may decide that she needs to change where she is worshipping and find a church that is more affirming of women.

The following is another conversation with our fictional Marie.

"Let's talk about your church, Marie," I said. "How are you feeling about worshipping there?"

"Well," Marie sighed, "There are lots of good things about it that I like. The music is great, and the people are generally pretty friendly. But they have this rule that women are not encouraged to share at the early service. In that service, people (by that I mean men) usually take turns standing up and reading from the Bible or sharing something that God has showed them that week, or they ask for a hymn to be sung. It is pretty low-key, and there are some men who clearly prepare ahead of time, and what they share really makes sense. But I feel they should allow the women to share as well, which they are debating now. They always said they didn't want women to share because they would take over, and then the men wouldn't want to share, but I don't think that would happen.

"I have a friend, Angela, who is a devoted Christian and is so knowledgeable about the Bible that she always has something worthwhile to say. Ironically, she is not allowed to speak, whereas some man can get up and repeat the same thing week after week. Anyway, you get the picture. Women are seen as the helpers, and men get the important jobs of preaching and teaching and being elders. The funny thing is that a lot of the women are okay with the system and think that those of us who want change are disruptive. But I think that things are gradually changing, so I will probably stick it out for now. I have started going to the evening service, and that is really good, and I do have several good friends. I do find that some of the women really get on my nerves when they talk about how wonderful their husbands are. One woman in my Bible study even shared that her husband was like Jesus to her. Please! My friend Judy and I just roll our eyes when she starts going on like that."

"It sounds like, despite the challenges, you are going to stay with your church for now?"

"Yes. Someone said there is no such thing as a perfect church, and if there was, it wouldn't be perfect once you joined it."

✿

A discussion as to whether an emotionally abused woman has healthy friends is also important, as abused women are often taken advantage of by other people outside the family. I would help the woman to evaluate her friendships and social relationships to see whether they were balanced and reciprocal or whether her friends were unhealthy as well. If that was the case, I would address that with her later, in the context of teaching assertiveness.

The work setting offers its own challenges, especially for highly sensitive women. Some of the women that came to me for counselling had the misfortune to have an employer who we discovered also had a narcissistic personality. Individuals with narcissistic personality disorder are extremely hard to work for, as they are generally critical and demanding and yet rarely offer any help to their staff. They prefer to hand over the mundane tasks to their employees and often have unrealistic expectations. On the other hand, they will take credit for the employees' hard work and claim it as their own. They require constant feeding of their egos, and if that does not happen, they will do their best to make life miserable for their employees. The saying "I don't get mad; I get even" applies to these individuals.

There are many examples of people in positions of authority and government leaders past and present who favour only those who give them wholehearted support and punish those who do not agree with them. The employee relationship is a difficult one, especially if a woman does not have many other options for employment.

If a woman in such a situation had an opportunity to change jobs, I would encourage her to consider that option, given that these individuals are unlikely to change over time. However, if she was only a few years from retirement or did not have other options, then I would encourage her to use the same assertive tactics that I would be teaching her shortly in terms of how to deal with a narcissistic spouse or parent.

Narcissistic male employers are notorious for inappropriate sexual advances in the workplace, as they have no respect for anyone working under them, especially women, and believe that they are so attractive that any woman would be thrilled with their advances. Sadly, many women have to choose between losing their jobs or putting up with sexually inappropriate behaviour. Nevertheless, if a woman in that work situation learns to be assertive and makes it clear she will not tolerate being disrespected, she may be able to continue in her job. Certainly, once she becomes more aware of the disordered individual's personality, she will be more able to notice red flags and take appropriate steps to protect herself. Her newfound knowledge will also be helpful if she starts interviewing for a new job because she will be able to recognize the subtle red flags early on in the interview process.

Once a woman has spent time evaluating the relationships in all the different settings in which she operates (home, work, church, friendships, and so forth), then she is ready to look at strategies to employ which will enable her to handle the unhealthy personalities in these various settings.

*Challenge her false beliefs and teach
relaxation techniques and mindfulness.*

M any emotionally abused women subscribe to mistaken beliefs
which are views and attitudes about themselves, others, and
the world that are not commonly shared by the majority of other
people. These mistaken beliefs have contributed to their low self-
esteem and have predisposed them to being taken advantage of
and emotionally abused by the various unhealthy people in their
lives.

Edmund J. Bourne's book *The Anxiety and Phobia Workbook*
(2020) is an excellent resource and has several chapters that
are very helpful. In one chapter, he sets out a mistaken beliefs
questionnaire, which I would often do in sessions with a
woman I was counselling. I would score it and then use it as a
jumping-off point to tackle specific mistaken beliefs. Doing this
often heightens a woman's awareness that she has beliefs about

herself and others that are not shared by the majority of the population. Until confronted with this directly in the form of a questionnaire, she has usually thought that most people shared her beliefs. I would point out that these mistaken beliefs were definitely contributing to her anxiety, depression, or low self-esteem and that we needed to challenge them. I would send each woman home with a copy of the book, which gives some good suggestions as to how to challenge the mistaken beliefs, and we would review these strategies in the session as well. I would also encourage her to read the chapter in Bourne's workbook about self-talk, and we would discuss how her internal dialogue had a significant effect on how she felt about herself and would impact her ability to handle stressful situations. If her self-talk consisted of many mistaken beliefs, then it was no wonder that she was experiencing significant stress in her life as she navigated her various relationships.

One of the barriers that emotionally abused people have in terms of learning assertiveness is that they subscribe to the mistaken belief that everyone should like them and that it is their job to make sure that happens.

They are afraid to say no to a request, because they believe the person making the request won't like them if they do so. Letting go of this mistaken belief is difficult because many abused women have been trained since childhood that they must always say yes so that their parents will love them. That view is very functional during childhood because it helps a child to survive and feel safe in an unhealthy environment. The child develops the skill of pleasing the disordered parent, and the parent may occasionally reward the child for that behaviour. The problem is that it is not our responsibility to make others happy; that is their job. But the disordered parent convinces the child that it is her job to please the parent. When the child is occasionally successful, it can engender a feeling of power, so the child holds on to the mistaken belief that she can make the parent happy. The child knows that if the parent is happy, then she will be safe and secure.

If this belief persists into adulthood, the woman may still believe that she needs to make other people happy in order to feel secure.

While this belief gave the child a fleeting sense of power, as an adult it becomes an overbearing burden (not to mention an impossible one).

I would often ask a woman in an abusive situation whether she liked everyone, to which she would generally answer no. I would then counter by asking her why she expected that everyone should like her. I would follow that up by asking the key question, which is "Why would you want an unhealthy person to like you?"

I would remind the woman I was counselling that when narcissistic individuals like someone, it is because that person is continuing to meet their needs. I would try to help her see that the only thing worse than the narcissist not liking her is the narcissist liking her, continuing to take advantage of her, and sucking her dry with constant demands. I would stress that it is preferable if unhealthy people dislike us, because then they leave us alone rather than demanding our time and attention trying to fill the bottomless pit of their needs. And because people with personality disorders are so self-focused, generally dominating the conversation, they are also very exhausting to be around. They can take up so much of our time and energy that we don't have time to cultivate or enjoy any healthy people in our lives.

The mistaken belief that everyone should like her also contributes to an abused woman's low self-esteem, as it naturally follows that everyone else's needs must take priority over hers. It also makes her more vulnerable to additional other unhealthy relationships, because other people see this trait and are happy to exploit it. Unfortunately for Christian women, this belief is often encouraged, as they are taught to put others ahead of themselves. It is interesting that the Bible verse "Love others as you love yourself" (Galatians 5:14 MSG) may be misinterpreted to mean that we are always to put others ahead of ourselves. But it means that we are to love others in the same *manner* as we love ourselves, not "instead of" or "more than."

Many abused women have a number of mistaken beliefs which may have been adaptive in childhood but are clearly problematic in adult relationships. They include the following:

1. My needs are not as important as those of other people.
2. If I couldn't trust my parents to meet my needs as a child, then I definitely can't trust anyone else to meet them.
3. If others can't meet my needs, it is better if I don't ask for my needs to be met.
4. If I don't ask for my needs to be met, eventually I can block out my own needs completely and act as if I don't have any needs.
5. My job in life is to meet other people's needs so they will be happy and like me, and then I will feel secure.

These mistaken beliefs lead to the triad of "Don't talk … Don't trust … Don't feel." If a woman learns early on that she is not allowed to talk about her needs, then that leads to mistrust of others as she concludes that they are not willing or able to meet her needs. That mistrust in turn leads to her suppressing her own needs such that she genuinely doesn't feel that she has any needs.

For many abused women, simply making a choice is not something they are used to doing. They have learned to defer the choice to their parent or abusive partner and simply go along with whatever the other person decides.

One exercise that I often gave a woman I was counselling at this stage was to practise making simple choices to discover what her preferences were. Previously when faced with a choice, she would usually say, "It doesn't matter to me … whatever he likes." Challenging the woman to identify her likes and dislikes is the beginning of recognizing that she has needs and that it is okay to express them. She can start by expressing the needs to herself and practising meeting her own needs. This is a foreign concept for many abused women who need practice in trying to figure out what they really want. It can be as simple as a food preference or engaging in an activity. Many women have been taught that any such choices are "selfish." With these women, I would talk about taking care of our own emotional needs in order that we can be healthy enough to take care of others who truly need and appreciate us.

Because the prospect of being assertive with others often provokes anxiety, I needed to give the woman some tools to tackle the expected initial anxiety that she might experience when she worked to change her behaviour.

There are many good resources for teaching people how to relax, and I would take time to show her how to practise relaxation techniques. Again, Bourne's *Anxiety and Phobia Workbook* has an excellent chapter on relaxation strategies, which I would suggest that she read and practise for homework after I guided her through them in a session.

Mindfulness is another excellent skill in quelling anxiety, and I would also take time in a session to use guided imagery to help her relax. I wanted her to have a simple tool that she could use at any point in her day when she started to feel anxious.

The following is an example of how I would approach this with our fictional Marie.

"Marie, can you tell me of a place where you felt completely and utterly relaxed?"

Marie thought for a moment and then said it would be at a cabin that belonged to her brother where she used to go by herself to get away from the stresses of her life.

"Marie," I said, "I want you to tell yourself a story in your head (not out loud) imagining a trip that you are making to that cabin. I want you to imagine all the details leading up to the trip, such as packing the car, driving, getting out and smelling the pine forest and listening to the birds, and then making yourself comfortable in an easy chair in the cabin with a cup of tea. I want you to make up a narrative with your eyes closed for about two minutes, and I will tell you when to stop. If you come to the end of your story before I tell you to open your eyes, just repeat the story again in your mind."

Marie closed her eyes, and I timed a span of two minutes. "Okay, you can open your eyes now," I told her. "How do you feel?"

"I feel really relaxed. I always loved going there, and it was so peaceful just remembering how everything felt."

In most cases when I did this exercise with a woman, she would say she felt relaxed, and I would remind her that her feeling of relaxation followed from her thoughts, thus reinforcing the view that her thoughts had the power to change her emotions. I would also reinforce the view that the mistaken beliefs that she had been focusing on in her mind were contributing to her feelings of anxiety, and when she replaced them with calming thoughts, her anxiety would lessen. I would ask her to practise her own unique story until she could review it in her head whenever she was feeling anxious. Even in a work setting, she could take a minute or so to calm herself with this technique prior to handling a stressful situation. Once she was able to develop this skill, we would move to the next step of learning assertiveness.

Teach assertiveness in workplace
and personal relationships.

The key to a woman letting go of fear and anger toward her abusive partner as well as abusive family members, friends, and employers is assertiveness. Women who remain in abusive relationships are almost inevitably underassertive, which allows the abuse to continue.

With a Christian woman, I remind her of Ephesians 4:15, where Paul says, "God wants us to grow up, to know the whole truth and tell it in love." Most Christians have trouble combining those two. Either they withhold the truth out of "love" or they speak the truth without love.

There are three primary ways of responding to disrespect or abuse: aggressive, assertive, or underassertive. Aggressive people usually speak the truth about their feelings, but since they do so in anger, they are usually tuned out. On the other hand, underasservtive people may be very loving but are often afraid to speak the truth. They say yes when they should say no, and they don't speak the truth about their feelings. Ironically, neither the aggressive nor the underasservtive person actually gets heard. Most emotionally abused women fall into the underasservtive category, with occasional forays into the aggressive category, neither of which works when dealing with unhealthy people.

Assertive people speak the truth about what they are feeling, or want, but they do it with kindness and respect. Because of this approach, they are usually listened to. They don't get walked on like underasservtive people or feared or avoided like aggressive people.

There are many good books on teaching people assertiveness, and I would typically send the woman I counselled home with one to read and grasp the concepts that she would need to apply as she learned to deal with her abuser. An excellent book now in its tenth edition is *Your Perfect Right* by Allerti and Emmons. Another helpful resource is the updated Cloud and Townsend book *Boundaries*, which has become a classic in the field.

Learning assertiveness is primarily learning how to say no. The beginning step is for the woman to give herself some time before she responds with either yes or no to a request. She needs to say, "Let me think about that, and I will get back to you." Or she can say, "Let me check my calendar, and I will call you back." Even if it is only a few minutes, she is giving herself a chance to think through the request before responding.

A woman learning assertiveness should ask herself several questions prior to responding to a request to determine whether saying yes to the request is the correct response or whether her response should be no.

I suggest the following questions:

1. "Do I have the skill to do this?" (Generally, the answer is yes, but it is important that the woman be honest about her own limitations.)

2. "Do I have the time to do this?" Given that God gives us all the same twenty-four hours every day, the question then becomes "If I say yes to this request, what do I have to say no to?" The no may be taking time for herself or doing something she has been putting off. This question forces her to realize that if she does say yes, it replaces something else currently on her calendar.

3. "Do I have joy in doing this?" Obviously, this does not apply to requests that are part of the woman's job, but rather requests coming from family members or friends. The question of whether the task is a burden needs to be addressed.

4. "Is there someone else who should be doing this task?" Again, this may refer to the person who is doing the asking. It is important not to be doing something for someone that he or she is capable of doing but just wants someone else to do it.

5. "Is there any downside to saying yes to this request?" Perhaps there are other people who would enjoy being asked, and they will not have the chance to be helpful if she takes over and does this.

The last two questions are often applicable to parents who are teaching their children mastery over a particular skill. But it applies equally to unhealthy people who try to manipulate others out of arrogance or laziness.

If the woman determines that she has the skill, time, and joy to do the task, and if there is no downside, then of course she can answer yes. However, if not, then she needs to say no.

There are many different ways of saying no, all of which are polite and respectful. Some women mistakenly believe that saying no is harsh and rejecting, but it can be done with respect for the other person. Learning the various ways of saying no helps the woman let go of any guilt that she may previously have felt about turning down a request.

It is important to preface saying no with a statement that validates the person's feelings, such as "I understand that you would like me to do such and such …" But just because we understand their feelings does not mean that we agree to the request.

The first type of no is the delayed no. This no is used in response to being asked to do something right away. The response can be "No, I am sorry, I can't do that right now, but I do have some time tomorrow [or next week]." With this no, the woman has decided to agree to the request, but she chooses when she is going to do what has been requested. She is taking control and choosing a time that works for her.

The second type of no is the partial no. This is the assertive response when the woman is asked to do a whole task but time or other issues prevent her from taking all of it on herself. An example might be if the woman is asked to chair a committee.

Her response can be "No, I can't commit to being the chair, but I would be happy to be on the committee." In this situation, the woman decides what part of the task she has the time and energy to commit to.

The third type of no is the helpful no. This response is best when doing the task would prevent the other person from taking responsibility or learning a new skill. An example would be "No, I can't do that for you, but I would be happy to show you how to do it."

The fourth type of no is the referral no. In this case, the women offers an alternative suggestion. She may say, "I can't do that for you, but I think so and so would be able to help you," or "I can send you a website for you to check out some possibilities."

The fifth type of no is the final no. This no is used when the woman can't do it later, can't help with part of it, and can't help the person do it or suggest an alternative option. This no can still be respectful and kind. An example would be to say, "No, I can't help you with that, but" and follow that with one of the following responses:

- "I am confident you can manage."
- "I believe that you will be able to find someone else to help you."
- "I believe it would be helpful for you to learn to do that yourself."
- "I will pray that you will find a solution to your problem."

It is also important for the woman to realize that, contrary to what the person asking may assume, she does not need to give an explanation as to why she is saying no.

Women often feel that they are obliged to give a plausible excuse as to why they are saying "no to a request. They are not. In fact, the woman often sets herself up to be manipulated when she does offer an excuse, as the person making the request can then find a way to cajole her into doing the task. For example, if the woman says, "No, I can't drive you to the mall this morning, because I am taking my child to the doctor," the other person can respond, "Oh, no problem, just drop me on the way."

Unhealthy personalities believe that they are owed an explanation for why the woman can't do what they have asked. Again, rather than giving specific reasons, it is better if the woman just says something vague or general, such as "That doesn't work for me." If the person persists and asks, "Why?" the woman can just say, "It just doesn't."

This "broken record" technique is a hallmark of assertiveness.

Again, in most cases a final "no" response needs to be prefaced by saying, "I understand that you are unhappy that I can't do this," which tells the other person that you understand his or her feelings. However, the key is not to give in and agree to the request.

Assertiveness is a key skill for an emotionally abused woman to have in dealing with unhealthy personalities, as their requests are often unfair, untimely, and burdensome.

The workplace offers its own unique challenges. Unfortunately, fear of workplace reprisals prevents some women from being as assertive as they need to be. Many underassertive women end up saying nothing and essentially teach their bosses that they will stay late and work overtime to reach an unrealistic goal. This pretty much ensures that they will be asked again. In the workplace, underassertive people are usually liked but not respected, so if a woman is also caught up in being liked, then she will pay the price of exhaustion and having no personal or family time.

While it is not possible for a woman to say no to a boss who is loading her down with excessive work, it is possible to ask the boss to prioritize the new request with the existing workload. For example, if the woman's boss suddenly drops a new task on her desk and wants it done right away, a good strategy is for the woman to say, "I will be happy to do that, but you need to tell me which of my existing tasks you want me to postpone, because I will not have time to do all of them today."

At no time is the woman to speak with any negative tone in her voice that would communicate anger or frustration. She should simply state that if she takes on a new task, one of the other tasks needs to be put aside. She may even be able to use humour (e.g., by saying, "I know you think I am Superwoman, and I wish I were, but I don't want to rush and do a poor job that would reflect badly on you and the company").

Once the woman I was counselling had practiced assertiveness in her workplace situation, we would move to the key area of personal relationships. I would remind her that the goal with unhealthy family members is to teach them to respect her. If respect from family members is accompanied by dislike, that dislike can be reframed as a good thing because it generally means they will give up trying to manipulate her into doing what they want, granting her more freedom in her life.

At this point I would also spend time explaining the difference between reacting and responding. Typically, the woman would describe waiting on tenterhooks for the unhealthy parent or partner to say something rude and then either shutting down or "reacting emotionally." Reacting is quick and emotional, whereas responding is measured, calm, and planned ahead of time. Preparing a response means that whatever the abuser says, the woman will have her standard reply ready. Saying no to someone with an unhealthy personality is often going to be met with negativity. A healthy person who respects boundaries will perhaps be disappointed when told no but will accept that the other person has the right to say no. On the contrary, the unhealthy personalities will often become angry because, with their sense of entitlement, they do expect the other person will meet their needs. Again, a response such as "I am sorry that you are disappointed, but unfortunately I am not able to help you" acknowledges the frustration but does not result in capitulation and doing what the other person asks. In fact, saying no to someone is often a good test of how emotionally healthy that person actually is.

While saying no often means the abuser will be unhappy, if the woman has grasped the idea that it is not her job to make the other person happy, and if she has said no with respect and kindness, then she need not feel guilty.

I would explain to the woman that assertiveness takes practice and that it initially may feel uncomfortable for her to say no. I would encourage her to write out typical scenarios in which she anticipates someone asking her to do something and then crafting a response. She could then memorize her response or write it down and even post it next to her phone so she would be prepared for the next time she had contact with the unhealthy person.

Humour is something that I sometimes recommend women use when they are dealing with criticism from an abusive person. One very bright woman I worked with was very accomplished in her various charitable and professional committees, but her husband criticized almost everything she did. At one point she was slicing up some cheese to wrap their cat's pills in it, and her husband told her she was cutting the cheese wrong. She looked at him and said, "It must be awful for you to have a wife whom you believe can't even slice cheese." He looked at her in astonishment and was loath to criticize her again.

One woman's mother was very critical of the length of her hair and said curtly, "Did you mean to get it cut that short?"

A possible response could be, "Yes, but the good news is that my hair grows so quickly it will be back to a length that you like by next week."

In response to being told that she looked as if she had put on weight, another woman told her mother, "I know. I wish I could afford a gym membership. Do you think you could give me one for my birthday?"

Typically, the person making the criticism is taken aback and rendered speechless when these techniques are used, especially if the woman uses another effective technique, which is agreeing with the criticism.

As an example, if a woman is told, "You are so dumb; I can't believe you forgot that again," her response can be, "You are absolutely right! I don't think you should ask me to do that any more." The point of using humour is for the woman herself to see the situation as ludicrous and to laugh at herself in such a way that the abuser has no comeback. Such responses are better options to the usual response to criticism, which is to deny, argue, make excuses, or remain silent, none of which work with an abusive individual.

With unhealthy family members, using assertiveness may come with the risk of the abuse escalating initially, and so the woman has to be prepared for attempts to manipulate her using guilt. Narcissistic parents have been known to respond by complaining that they are about to die or saying that they will cut the adult child out of their will, and this can trigger a woman's sense of guilt. If the parent is elderly and needs support, this is a special challenge. Often these elderly parents are very dependent on the woman for running errands, cooking, cleaning, or keeping them company, all the while complaining and treating her with rudeness and disrespect. I have discovered the irony that often the more unhealthy the parent is, the more devoted the adult child. This is where the same guilt that the parent used to control the child still influences the adult woman to try to meet her parent's needs. For other women, their unrealistic "hopefulness" motivates them to continue to try and please the elderly parent.

At this stage I would take time to explain to a woman in this situation the principle of variable reinforcement and how powerful it is. This is the principle exploited by all gambling sites. According to the principle, whether a behaviour is successful in achieving a desired reward is completely unpredictable. The gambler may win once and then not again for fifteen tries, or he may win once and then again the second time. This type of variable reinforcement (or reward) is very powerful in motivating people to continue their same behaviour. I explain that even if the woman says no to abusive behaviour twenty times and then gives in once, she will have undone the initial twenty times. She must persist in being assertive until the unhealthy person gets the message that he or she cannot manipulate her.

I also remind a woman in such a situation that this is also the reason why she herself keeps hoping that the parent will treat her kindly. On occasion, the parent will pop up to normal and relate in a pleasant way, and that keeps the woman hooked in, believing that she is in control of the situation.

I often ask a woman who is continuing to be abused by an elderly parent whether there is anything that parent could do that would be worse than what he or she did to the woman as a child. Often the woman will be taken aback and admit that nothing done to her now could be worse than what she suffered as a child. Then I ask, "If that is so, then what is it that you fear if you are assertive with your parent now?" She will often say, "She will get angry at me." I then explore with her the consequences of the parent getting angry. If she says that the parent won't talk to her, then I remind her that she can view that as a vacation from having to meet the parent's needs or visit him or her. I remind the woman that she is not a helpless little girl any more and that she needs to experience her parent's anger as a signal to remind the parent to respect her or to leave the situation.

The latter option of removing herself from the abusive situation with a disordered parent is an important one. She can leave the room or even hang up the phone if the parent is being rude to her. I stress that there is no point in getting angry at the parent or speaking in a rude tone of voice. Instead, when the parent is speaking to her in a rude tone of voice or criticizing her, then a better option is to simply say, "I am finding this conversation too stressful, so I will need to take a break and get back to you later."

It is important that, having said that, she either leave the room or hang up the phone to reinforce her words. The woman needs to use "I" messages rather than blaming or criticizing the parent. She needs to simply say that she personally is feeling stressed, which the parent usually can't dispute.

A disordered parent will generally test out whether he or she can still manipulate the woman, but if the woman is calm and persistent, eventually the parent will realize that if he or she wants the woman to visit or phone (and disordered parents generally do), he or she will need to start treating her better.

Another challenge for abused women is the situation where the parent plays the victim and starts bemoaning how badly he or she is being treated. Rather than becoming defensive, the woman can simply say, "I hear what you are saying, but I am not comfortable listening to that, so I will come back when you are in a better mood." It is quite striking how quickly even elderly parents can learn new rules if the woman persists in being in the parent's company only when the parent is speaking respectfully and not complaining.

One woman tried this assertive approach with her parents who, whenever she came to visit, would shout at each other and argue the whole time. The woman told me how stressed she was sitting there listening to them fight. On my suggestion, at the next visit the woman explained to her parents that listening to them fight was too stressful for her and that she would have to leave if they continued. Interestingly, they quickly learned to keep the conversation calm when she was around.

Because most abused women are able to predict what the disordered parent is likely to say or complain about, I would often role-play a script of what a woman I was counselling needed to say in return. I would then play the role of the critical parent, and she would practise an assertive response.

In addition to challenging disrespectful behaviour, we would review situations when the parent popped up to normal and was polite. In those circumstances, I would encourage the woman to give her parent lots of praise and thus reward the good behaviour. Because disordered parents love praise and attention, I would suggest that the woman give the parent much more attention when he or she was behaving properly and then withdraw that attention when the parent reverted to his or her critical self. If this is done consistently, the parent will eventually learn to modify his or her behaviour when the woman is present.

I would remind the woman that it was essential that everyone in her life treat her with respect, both for herself and also as an example for her children. If her children saw her being treated disrespectfully, they would likely end up treating her disrespectfully as well. If her adult children were treating her with disrespect, we needed to work on that as well. This is not uncommon if the children have watched their mother being treated badly by their father. Sometimes a child may identify with the mother and stand up to the father, but more likely he or she will see the mother as weak and begin to treat her disrespectfully as well.

In instances where the adult children are living elsewhere, a woman experiencing abuse can use the same technique of leaving or hanging up the phone if they are rude to her; however, it is more problematic if they are living at home. Most parents are okay to subsidize an adult child living with them if that child is attending school or college, but if they are neither at school nor working and not paying rent, then tough love needs to happen. An adult child needs to be doing something productive to warrant free room and board past a certain age. Sadly, if the mother has been overly accommodating, it will be hard to persuade the adult child to take over meeting his or her own needs. The woman will need to stop providing an easy life to persuade him or her to move out.

In some cases, it may be necessary for the woman to set up her adult children in their own apartment, move them in, pay the first month's rent, and then leave them to face the normal responsibilities of adulthood. I remember one extreme case in which the mother simply could not dislodge her two narcissistic adult children from the home. Eventually she herself moved out and rented an apartment and left them to manage without her.

On a more positive note, it has been my experience that if the woman does a reasonable job of teaching her children to respect her, they will eventually begin to treat her with respect. Often, they will come around to seeing the reality of the situation and recognize that their mother has been abused. Usually this happens after a separation when their father starts showing his true colours to them and they bear the brunt of his disordered personality. At that stage, and it may take several years, it is more likely that the woman's adult children will start to realize what their mom went through and develop compassion for her. It is important for the woman to wait until her adult children come to their own conclusion rather than try to get them to take sides. Regardless of whether the adult children see the abusiveness clearly, it is important for the woman to teach her children that she deserves their respect both as their mother and as a human being. She needs to practise the same assertiveness skills with her adult children that she does with anyone else.

My now deceased mother-in-law gave me ample opportunity to practise these assertiveness strategies. First of all, it was very helpful for me to recognize that she had classic narcissistic traits. That enabled me to let go of any expectation that she would be able to make significant changes in her behaviour. When she was eventually moved into a nursing home, she constantly complained about her roommate within earshot on the other side of the curtain. Her roommate was a sweet old lady whom I would say hello to as well. My mother-in-law was very resentful of any attention being diverted from her and made critical comments about her roommate. At one point I told her that unless she could say something positive about her roommate, I did not want to hear anything. She knew that if she didn't make some changes, my visit with her in the nursing home would be cut short and I would simply leave. Given that there were almost no other visitors, this was a good motivator for her. At one point I could tell she was about to start complaining about her roommate, but she bit her lip instead.

Now let's see how our fictional Marie is doing.

"Well, Marie," I said, "are you ready to practise being assertive with your dad?"

"I think so," she replied. "I have been assertive with Steve, and that has been going well."

"Tell me about that," I said.

"Well, I did what you suggested, which was to tell Steve that if he started to complain about me, it would probably be better if he did the job himself.

"At first he just groaned and asked why he had to do everything, and I just told him it was because he was so much better at it than I was. I think he was surprised, but he couldn't back down because of his ego. So he has been helping out more with Stevie, and when he does, I give him lots of praise and thanks and tell him what a great dad he is. I think he likes that, plus I noticed that he is bragging to his mom about all that he is doing, and she praises him too. I don't think his dad did very much, so maybe he didn't have a good role model.

"He was in a bad mood last week, and I just handed Stevie to him and said that I was too stressed to listen any more and that I needed to go for a walk to calm down. When I got back, I think he was glad to hand Stevie back to me, because he had pooped his diaper.

"It is funny that when I felt I was ready to be assertive with Steve, it went better than I expected. I think he sensed that I wasn't going to put up with his moods any more."

"So let's plan what you are going to say to your dad," I said.

"Well, I want to ask him if it is okay if Mom comes over to be with Stevie."

"Wait a minute," I said. "It is not a question of asking him if it is okay, because then he can say no. You need to simply tell him what is going to happen."

"You mean just tell him that we are going to pick Mom up and drive her to our place?"

"Absolutely," I said.

"But what if he says no?," Maria asked.

"Simply tell him it is not negotiable. Do you really think he is going to leave work and come home and chain her to the kitchen table so she can't leave?"

"Well, no, he wouldn't take time away from his work."

"Exactly. Remember it will go better if you can find a way to validate him in this whole discussion."

"I guess I could tell him that we want Stevie to have the same good experience that he had with his grandmother," Marie said. "He was close to her, and she spoiled him."

"Perfect. That is a good way to help him see it in a different light."

"Okay, I will talk to him when we drop over this evening. The good thing is that Steve is also on board with this, and so I think Dad will back down if he sees that. Other times it seemed like it was him and Steve against me. Steve doesn't have any trouble being assertive, so I think it will go okay."

⚜

Now let's check in with Stella to see how she is doing with being assertive.

⚜

"Hi Stella," I said as she walked into my office for our next session. "Did you get a chance to practise assertiveness with Alex?"

"Not yet," she said. "I decided to practise it on my mom first."

"How did it go?" I asked.

"Well, it was really interesting," Stella replied. "Remember how I told you how she and Alex always get along so well? Well, she asked me to drive her for groceries, and I was really busy, so I said, 'Why don't you ask Alex? I'm sure he would be happy to drive you.'

"She was surprised but decided to phone him instead, and he just gave her the runaround. I called him and said that I was sure he would want to help her out after all she had done for him, but he just said it was my job and there was no way he was going to help her out."

"When I told her that, I could tell that she was taken aback; but rather than ask me again, she found someone else to help her. I was dumbfounded, as she always said she had no one but me to help her, but apparently her neighbour pitches in at times. Anyway, after this I feel much better saying no to her, because I know she can get other people to do things for her if I can't. Funnily enough, after Alex turned her down, she hasn't been as responsive to his requests for money. I think she is beginning to see my side of things more.

"I also told her that I didn't want to listen to her complain about how I do things, because it was too stressful, and she actually said that she never complains about me. I was so taken aback that I blurted out, 'Yes you do. You tell me I fold laundry wrong, that my casserole was too spicy, that my kids aren't polite enough.' I wasn't really angry; I was just so shocked that she seemed oblivious to how critical she is."

"How did she respond to that?" I asked.

"Well, of course she couldn't apologize, because according to her she is never wrong, but she has been nicer to me lately.

"I have also been doing that thing you suggested when she starts going on about how ill she is. I simply say I can't listen to that any more, as it is too stressful for me. I have noticed that she doesn't go on and on about her ailments as much any more.

"I used to make excuses for her with my kids when they would ask why she was so rude to me by saying she was just not feeling well, whereas now I just tell them that she is not a healthy personality but we don't have to take it personally. I tell them that the reason she doesn't want to spend time with them is nothing to do with them but is because she just wants people to listen to her talk about herself. I think they were relieved—especially my son, as he is really sensitive.

"I think I was always afraid that if I didn't do what she wanted, she would get angry and cut me off, but now I see that is not necessarily a bad thing. Maybe I was caught up in thinking I was so important to her and that she really needed me, and that made me feel good. But now I see she can manage to get other people to meet her needs if I can't, so I don't need to take on that whole burden myself."

"Good for you, Stella!" I exclaimed. "That is wonderful news."

Stella came in the following week looking discouraged, so I asked her what happened when she tried out her assertiveness skills with Alex.

"He just flew into a rage," Stella replied. "He ranted on about how he has been putting up with me for years and how I am the one abusing him and he has had enough and if I don't like it, then I can just pack up and leave because it is his house and he is not going to be the one to leave."

"Oh dear, Stella, I am so sorry," I said. "How did you respond to that?"

Well, I told him that I was tired of him blaming me for everything and that things had to change, but it was so awful I just ended up crying and going to my room."

"Okay, Stella, we need to look at your options so you can choose the course of action that you feel most comfortable with," I said.

9

*Assist her in the decision to stay or
leave the abusive marital situation.*

O nce the woman experiencing abuse has developed good
assertiveness skills, she is in a position to make a key decision
as to whether to stay in the marriage or leave. In some cases, the
decision may become obvious over time. If the woman becomes
more assertive, then her abusive partner may choose from two
different options.

He may decide that since she is no longer meeting his needs,
he will end the relationship and get his needs met elsewhere. He
may be doing this already by having affairs, viewing pornography,
lying, and spending money they don't have. If the abuser himself
decides to leave, it can make things a little easier for the woman.
Generally, narcissists don't leave until they have found someone
else to fulfil their needs. They like to have a backup in the
wings and so often already have someone else in mind to fill the

bottomless pit of their needs. It is ironic, but the best thing that can happen to an abused woman if she wants to end the marriage is for her partner to find someone else.

Sadly, there is generally no opportunity for the woman to warn the "new" woman in her husband's life about the brevity of the honeymoon stage. Even if given the chance, she will not be believed if the new woman is being blinded by the narcissist's initial charm.

If the abuser himself decides to leave, it means that he takes the initiative rather than the woman herself. This doesn't mean, however, that he doesn't lay the blame for all the problems on her. In one case that I dealt with, the narcissistic husband pre-emptively met with all of the woman's own relatives, seeking sympathy and telling them what a terrible wife she was. Given how convincing this abuser was, it was a terrible blow to the woman to discover that her own family members actually believed her partner's lies about her.

But what if the abuser refuses to leave the marriage? Then the decision is up to the woman to decide whether to stay or go. Not all women who are married to disordered personalities make the decision to leave their marriages.

For a woman who is completely financially dependent on her partner, the decision to leave comes with additional stress in that she may need to get back into the workforce, downsize her home, and possibly relocate to a less expensive area. All of these stresses are also borne by the children, and so the woman may decide that it is simply exchanging one set of problems for a new set and choose to stay. If the children are younger and she needs the stability of a marriage and financial support, she may decide to stay until the children are out of the home. She may make this decision in order not to disrupt her children's lives, which will certainly happen in a divorce, as she will almost inevitably be financially worse off.

If a woman I was counselling decided to stay, I would work with her around protecting herself from abuse. It is really important for a woman who decides to stay in an emotionally abusive relationship to use her newfound assertiveness skills to protect herself and her children, and to model asking for respect for the sake of her children as well as herself.

The first thing that the woman needs to put in place is a way of escaping temporarily when things get worse (which they frequently will). She needs to have a plan to get away for an evening or weekend when the abuse gets really bad. Enlisting the aid of a healthy friend who will support her in this is essential. If a family member is on her side, she needs to know that in an emergency she can arrive on that person's doorstep. Sometimes this is hard, as many abuse victims are too ashamed to confide in family members about the abuse they are suffering, and so it may come as a surprise when she shares with them. Once she has a plan and the abuser won't stop harassing her, she needs to get in her car and drive to her safe place or call a friend to pick her up. If she doesn't have a safe person to go to, then going to the library or mall are other alternatives. In any case, she needs to have an escape plan before she begins to practise her assertiveness on her partner.

The second thing that the woman needs to do is evaluate her financial situation. It is likely that her abuser controls the money, but if she is also employed, then she needs to set up her own bank account and keep an emergency fund in the event that she has to move out at some point in the future. She may need to park some money with a trusted family member or friend in the event that her spouse decides to empty their joint account. Once the woman has put in place some protective strategies and is confident that she could leave, this plan may give her the confidence to try and remain in the marriage.

If the woman decides to try to stay, the focus then shifts to helping her learn how to manage being in a relationship with someone who has a narcissistic personality disorder.

At this point in the counselling, she likely will have accepted that her partner won't change his thinking or suddenly be able to love her. But she can take steps to teach him to respect her. I tell women that it takes graduate-level assertiveness skills to live with and manage a disordered partner but that if she is determined, it is worth trying. Again, this presupposes that there is no physical abuse, sexual abuse, or coercive control; otherwise, the woman has no choice but to call the police and leave the situation.

There are ten rules that the woman must learn if she is to continue to live with her abuser. These rules apply not only to an abusive spouse but also to an abusive parent, adult child, or other relative.

1. *Don't debate, discuss, or defend (the three Ds).* Most narcissists label expressing a different opinion (i.e., a discussion) as a debate or argument. There is no point in arguing or debating with the abuser, but that doesn't mean that the woman has to go along with what he is asking her to do. She can practise the various ways of saying no mentioned earlier.

It is also important that she not be defensive in responding to the narcissist. It is natural for her to try and defend herself when she is being attacked, but if she is defensive, the narcissist will simply conclude that she is guilty.

2. *Rather than discussing or debating with him or becoming defensive, simply agree with the feeling behind what he is saying (e.g., "It must be frustrating for you that I am not doing what you want").* She can truthfully say to the abuser, "I understand how you are feeling," since she has researched the personality disorders. However, validating his feelings does not mean that the woman gives in and does what he is asking.

3. *Praise him when he behaves in a normal, helpful way.* This is very important because the narcissist loves praise and will sometimes repeat the behaviour if he gets enough positive strokes for doing it. Again, the woman needs to take advantage of the times when her partner pops up to normal and enjoy them, while not expecting that he will remain there.

4. *Be thankful for what he can do, and try to keep the focus on that.* The man will appreciate being thanked for the same thing over and over (such as bringing home a paycheck or buying the woman something). Most narcissists are obsessed with money, and this is the only way that they can feel loved, so they assume that buying gifts will make a woman feel loved. Ironically, most women would prefer that their partners would just listen and talk with them, providing an emotional connection. Since narcissists can't do that, they buy gifts to convince themselves and the

women that they are good partners, or to get something from the women. A woman in a relationship with a narcissist needs to accept the tangible gifts and be thankful for them, as these are often the only things the narcissist can really give his partner.

5. *Stop doing things for him that he can do for himself.* This may be difficult, as the man may often hand over to his partner anything that he doesn't want to have to do. But the woman can say, "I just feel you would do a better job of that than I would" or "I am sure you will figure that out."

6. *Decide what she will or won't do to meet his needs in the relationship.* For example, if both partners are working and the woman is the one doing all the cleaning, then she might say, "I know you want a clean house, but I am not able to keep it to your standards, so would you be able to help out, or should we hire a cleaning lady?" Or, if he is constantly complaining about her cooking, she can say, "I know you don't like a lot of what I prepare, so I think that on the weekends I will just cook what I want, and you can do the same."

7. *Remember that she cannot tell him what to do but can tell him only what she will or won't do.* This may include chores that the woman has ended up doing because the man conveniently "forgets" to do them. If she stops doing some chores, she will have to be okay with waiting for him to do them, because if she picks up the slack, he knows that he just has to wait her out.

8. *At all times, interact with him in a calm, pleasant tone of voice.* The woman cannot sound angry or upset and needs to

convey to the man that she is content with whatever he offers her.

9. *Do not ask for things that she knows from experience he is unable to do, such as provide emotional support when she is upset.* The woman needs to develop and count on her healthy friendships outside the home to meet her emotional needs rather than hoping that the man will meet those needs. She needs to be emotionally independent from him so she will not be disappointed when he fails to meet her needs. She needs to see her relationship with God as the source of all her needs.

10. *If these strategies fail, she needs to remove herself from the abusive situation physically.* The woman can go for a walk or drive, visit a friend, or do something that takes her out of the house and away from the verbal attacks. If the abuser questions her, she can reply, "It seemed like you were getting angry at me, so I thought it would be better if we had a break. I am happy to talk to you when you calm down." If she absents herself whenever the abuse escalates, then it gives the abuser the message that she is not going to tolerate it any more. Ironically, the abuser often hates being ignored, and so this strategy can work in her favour if she uses it judiciously.

In some cases, the abuser realizes that he does not benefit if his wife continues to remove herself from his presence whenever he treats her badly. If that is the case, then purely out of self-interest, he may choose to treat her with more respect. In those situations, the woman needs to see those times of normality as treats and enjoy them but not get her hopes up that they will continue uninterrupted. She needs to be able to be content with these small gains and not keep hoping for something more.

If the woman follows these rules with the abuser and she is able to maintain a degree of happiness and contentment in her life, then she may be able to stay in the relationship. For some women whose emotional needs are met by God and their friends and other family members, living with the abuser can become more neutral, if not happy. However, if even with practising all these rules the abuser still persists in his old ways, then she may have to reconsider her decision to stay. The decision to stay is often easier if the woman is not a highly sensitive person.

The decision to stay or go will also depend on the woman's support network. If she has a few good, healthy friends that she can talk to, or even get away with for a weekend, that may enable her to stay. If she has a job that she enjoys, then the balance of having a healthy work environment may also give her the emotional strength to tolerate an abusive home environment. At this stage, I help the woman evaluate the levels of stress in the other areas of her life in addition to her work. If she enjoys spending time with her children and can do that independently from her husband, then that may counterbalance what she has to put up with in her marriage.

If the abuse escalates when the woman practises assertiveness with her partner to the point where her emotional and psychological health are at stake, then the option of leaving the marriage needs to be discussed.

For many Christians, the option of leaving a marriage is acceptable only if there has been adultery or physical abuse. For the most part, Christian women who report physical abuse are believed and supported within the Christian community, as opposed to the women who are suffering emotional abuse and have no physical evidence of injuries. As I mentioned previously, none of the women in my practice reported any physical abuse, as that is not typical of narcissistic personalities. Many of the women were aware that their husbands were unfaithful but often were reluctant to share that information with others even though it was a key contributing factor in their emotional abuse.

It has been my experience that for Christian women, leaving a marriage is a last resort after other options have been tried and failed. If the woman makes the decision that her emotional and spiritual health has become too damaged to continue in the marriage, then we look at the risks that leaving entails. I explain to the woman that attempting to leave a relationship with someone who has a narcissistic personality is a very difficult task. If the woman leaves the abuser, then he will suffer a "narcissistic injury to his ego" and he will seek to punish her for leaving him.

Because money is very important to the narcissist, he will use money as his weapon to fight against what he perceives as his partner's betrayal in leaving the marriage. He will lie about his assets, hide money, and negotiate the lowest possible financial support as his way of punishing her for having the audacity to leave him. This is true even if he has been the one to be unfaithful to her. If a woman decides to leave her abuser, she needs to be prepared to suffer a significant financial loss. This is not welcome news, especially to a highly sensitive woman who has a strong sense of fairness and justice. First of all, when the woman announces her plan to leave the marriage, there will likely be a "honeymoon" period during which the man says he will change his behaviour, make all sorts of promises, and be on better behaviour. Unfortunately, it usually doesn't last, although it may delay the woman's decision to leave for several more months.

Once the abusive partner realizes that the woman is definitely going to leave, he will become very angry and do everything in his power to punish her for leaving him. He will fight tooth and nail to make sure that he comes out on top as far as finances go. This may include tactics such as refusing to co-sign to sell their home, spending money in the lead-up to the separation rather than having it go to her, hiding assets, and lying to her and his lawyer about his income. This is why the woman needs to try and get access to his income tax and banking records before she tells him she is leaving. Once he knows the marriage is over, he will take steps to prevent her from accessing this information.

Issues of child support payments are based on the man's income, but even when court ordered, the abuser will often refuse to pay. Some will go so far as to quit their jobs, declare bankruptcy, or even relocate to avoid paying anything. This is especially true of spousal support, which the abuser really does not want to pay. Here, too, a court order is rarely followed, and the woman often ends up trying to sue for spousal support—a situation that can take months or years.

Because of this, I urge the woman to try and negotiate a lump-sum settlement that doesn't involve her husband having to pay her any ongoing monthly support. If her husband has a pension, then she is entitled to half of that pension, and in those cases, it may be easier for her to get those benefits. If, however, her partner proposes that he send her a certain amount of money each month, that is not a good alternative, as he can stop at any time. I recommend that in the negotiating phase she begin by asking for things that she can withdraw later so as to ensure that he feels he has won.

Sometimes if the woman initially asks for spousal support, she can drop that request as a bargaining chip to secure some of the other assets. She needs to be aware that in most cases she must be seen to "lose" in the negotiation or the abuser will not sign the final papers. The narcissist will eventually settle if he believes that he has won, and the woman may well decide that, despite the financial cost, it is worth it emotionally for her to be free from an abusive relationship.

This brings up another important point in terms of the woman's choice of lawyers. Not all lawyers are assertive enough to deal with the machinations of the abuser, and in fact some will collude with him, believing his "poor me" stories.

In addition, if the woman's lawyer has never dealt with individuals with personality disorders, then she will not be able to provide the strong protection to her client that is needed. Her lawyer may believe that the husband is negotiating in good faith and inadvertently bias the agreement, especially if he is acting as his own lawyer. Given that many of these cases end up in court, the sad truth is that whoever has the better lawyer wins. And unfortunately, many abused women do not have the financial resources to hire the top guns in family law whose goal is to get as much as possible for their own clients. The adversarial nature of divorce court means that there will be winners and losers, and in almost all cases the women are the losers. This is also why I encourage women to try and settle first rather than go to court.

On a positive note, there are increasingly more family lawyers out there, as well as judges, who are becoming educated about personality disorders and the havoc that they wreak within the court system. One judge that I appeared before actually had his own copy of the DSM-5 to use as a reference.

If there are children involved, there are additional complications. The narcissist knows that he is obligated to pay child support, but he will tie that into access to the child, which may not be in the child's best interest or even what he himself wants.

In one case, a woman I saw was very troubled by the idea that her abusive husband would have unfettered access to her young daughter, and they went to court. After a two-year court battle in which the man fought for access, the court finally awarded him the access he asked for. He never saw the daughter again. For him it was all about his ego and the need to prove that he was a great father.

It is important for the woman to realize that if she leaves the marriage, her children will have a different relationship with her husband than she does. Sometimes a son will feel obliged to support his dad even if he knows it is not right. Interestingly enough, with many narcissistic fathers, when their wives leave, they turn their attention to their daughters to fill that void.

In one case, a woman told me that even though her husband had neglected their daughter for years, after the separation the husband suddenly paid lots of attention to the daughter. In that case, the daughter aligned herself with the dad out of feeling grateful for the unexpected attention she received. Sadly, sometimes a big reason for the woman deciding to stay in an abusive relationship is that she doesn't want the abuser to have unsupervised access to her children and wants to avoid the above problems.

Generally, young children may not fuss about having to go by themselves to visit Dad, but once the children get a little older, they may realize that Dad doesn't focus on them or even want them there. However, many narcissistic dads often push for a 50–50 custody arrangement where the child is with them for half the time simply so they don't have to pay the woman more child support. Most courts support a 50–50 custody split under the assumption that both parties are equally healthy, competent parents. Because a narcissist is generally a poor parent, he will often pawn the child off on the new woman in his life or on a grandparent rather than spending quality time with the child himself. Unfortunately, even when narcissists spend time with their children, it is on their terms, as they only want to do things with the children that they personally find enjoyable. They are not able to validate or accommodate a child who has interests different from their own.

Another problem that women with children face is that in some cases the children will blame the mother for the separation. Their lives have been disrupted, and they may not have some of the material things they want, and they see this as the mom's fault. Of course, this view is promoted by the dad who constantly tells the children that it was their mom who wanted the divorce. Again, this contributes to some women deciding to wait until the children are out of the home before making the decision to leave their partners.

Let's return to Stella to see how things are progressing with her.

⚜

"Well Stella," I said, "I think we need to go over your options in terms of staying with Alex or leaving him."

"I know," she replied. "I am so confused because, like I told you, he is really supported by the people at the church, and I know that I would be blamed if I left. He has just been so angry at me all the time. I realized that even if some of my church friends think it is wrong, I just can't live like this any more.

"He told me that if I leave him, he will go after my pension, as he doesn't have one because he was always being fired from his jobs. He knows he will get half of the house even though my parents paid for most of it as a wedding gift. He has really been turning on the charm with my family as well. My sister is divorced, and he is always over there helping her, and she thinks he is wonderful, so there is no point talking to her about how he treats me. Lately he has been extra nice to my daughter, and she is suddenly 'daddy's girl.' My son is pretty astute about people, and he sees what his dad is really like, so he doesn't say much, but I can tell he thinks I am being treated badly.

"Who do you have to help you out if you decide to leave?" I ask.

"Well, actually I have a few good friends from work, and they know what I have been going through. Oddly enough, my mom offered for me to stay with her, but that would be going from the frying pan into the fire, so I gently turned her down.

"I did talk to my pastor, and surprisingly he was pretty supportive, but he told me that God hates divorce and maybe Alex and I could just live separately for a period of time and see how that went. But I just want to have some closure so I can get on with my life. I want a more peaceful life where I am not stressed all the time. I have been putting up with him for the last twenty-five years, and it finally feels as if I can't do it any more. Lately when I pray, I feel that God is telling me that I don't need to bear this burden of an unhappy marriage any longer. I don't think I will ever remarry, but I just want to be free of the constant emotional abuse.

"I know that Alex is going to want to go after my pension, but I was thinking that maybe if we had an agreement where I gave him my half of the house in return for not touching my pension, he might go for that. He tends to like to have cash in his pocket, so that might work."

At our next session, I asked Stella whether her idea had worked out.

"What happened when you talked to Alex about separating?" I asked.

"Well, first I decided to try your strategy of agreeing with everything he said and even exaggerating it," Stella replied. "I told him that he was probably right and it wasn't fair that he had to put up with me and he deserved someone who could be a better wife to him. I told him I was sorry I couldn't be the wife he wanted and I wanted to give him his freedom to make a different choice. He was really dumbfounded, but he couldn't really back down. He just said that he wanted his 'fair share' of our assets, meaning most of everything. I pointed out that if I signed over my half of the house to him, then that would actually be more than the value of my pension and that way he would have more cash right now rather than waiting years for me to retire. He said he would think about it.

"Of course, he wanted all the best furniture to stay in the house, but he agreed I could take the kids' old bunk beds and an old sofa and table that we had in the rec room. He would have taken the dishes and silver that my mom had given us, but she said she wanted it back herself. He wanted my car, but it isn't paid off yet, so I told him that if I turned it over to him, he would have to pay the monthly payments, so he didn't like that plan. He said that he would just buy his own or borrow my sister's car as they are so friendly now. She even offered to have him stay with her if he decides to sell the house so he won't have to rush into buying something right away."

"Wow, that must have been hurtful," I said.

"Well, my sister is a lot like my mom, and so she and I have never been close. I think she has always been jealous of me for some unknown reason and this is her way of getting back at me. I am actually relieved that I don't have to look after Alex, because he is so high maintenance. My sister will discover that in time, but right now it means that the separation will go more smoothly because he can tell everyone that I was the bad guy and that even my sister is not supporting me."

"What about the folks at church?" I asked.

"Well, they have all rallied behind Alex, as I suspected would happen," said Stella. "But I am okay with that, because he is getting all this attention and support, so he is less likely to go after me and try to punish me like you said some abusers do. He is definitely the 'winner' in all of this, but I am okay with that, as I can just slip away and make a new life for myself."

"Where will you move to?" I asked.

"Well, a friend of mine has a basement apartment in her home, and she said the lease is up and when her tenant moves out next week, she will rent it to me if I want it. I can manage it on my salary, and she and I get along well, so it is a good plan for us both. She is divorced, and we spend a lot of time together anyway, so this way it will be good for us both."

"How are your kids taking the news?"

"Well, they are both going to be living on their own this fall. My son is going to move into residence, and he has a part-time job to cover his expenses. My daughter is going to work for a year and then probably take some courses at university, so they will both be okay. I have told them that they never have to choose between their dad and me, so if there is an event that we both want to attend, I will always be polite and courteous. My daughter said that it seems that Alex and my sister are an 'item,' as they call it now, and she thinks that is awful. My son doesn't want to get involved, so we don't talk about it much. They are both happy to come out for pizza with me on Sundays, so I am thankful for that. I know they will be moving on with their lives soon. I think it was a wake-up call for them in terms of realizing that I wasn't going to put up with the abuse any more, so they actually both treat me better than they used to."

"How do you feel about your decision to leave?" I asked.

"Well, I am a little sad at times because I hoped it would work out, but I am actually more relieved than sad. I will be okay on my own with God's help, even if some folks think I am making a mistake. I just feel like a huge burden has been lifted, and I am starting to make choices for myself and discovering what things I like and don't like. And now that my mom is treating me more respectfully, I feel like the future is brighter and I can handle what comes my way. The only thing I am worried about is repeating the same mistakes with whoever I meet in the future."

"Don't worry about that, Stella" I said. "We will tackle that next."

*Help her to make healthy choices
in future relationships*

T he final step is helping to prepare the abused woman for future
relationships by reviewing her new knowledge and putting it
into practice. She needs to look at the changes that she needs to
make within herself to become healthier so that she will attract
healthy people. Sometimes the woman would tell me that she
had no healthy friends at all. We would then examine why that
was, and often it was because she came across to people as a giver
who just wanted to help them and didn't need any help herself. In
healthy friendships, we want to be able to meet the other person's
needs at least some of the time, and so if a woman portrays herself
as just wanting to be the "giver" in a relationship, then potentially
healthy friends may give her a pass because they feel she would
not be open to accepting anything from them. As the old saying
states: If you love someone, you let them do for you." If a woman

gives off the impression that she has no needs and simply wants to be the helper, then the only people that will be attracted to her as a friend or partner will be the self-centred ones who are needy and want someone to fill those needs.

By the time a woman has reached this final step, she will have learned to identify and express her own needs and so should be able to share with others what she likes. This includes practising making choices and decisions founded on her new-found wisdom and emotions rather than her previous mistaken beliefs, as well as using her assertiveness skills to weed out unhealthy friends.

When the woman meets a potential new friend (whether male or female), I encourage her to follow some simple steps in terms of her own attitudes and behaviour:

1. She needs to hold back from offering to meet that person's needs right away to give herself time to see whether the person reaches out to her. She needs to ask herself questions like "Am I always the one to call the other person, or do they take the initiative to call me?"

2. She needs to pay attention to how she feels in the company of that person. Is she able to relax and be herself, or does she feel she is walking on eggshells?

3. She needs to ask herself whether she feels exhausted or energized after spending time with a prospective new friend. If she is feeling exhausted, it is likely a sign that the relationship is not balanced and she would be better off not pursuing it.

4. She needs to practice being okay if the other person doesn't like it when she is assertive, and see it as God directing her to move on from that relationship.

5. She needs to curb her natural tendency to want to develop a deep relationship too soon. She needs to slow down and take time to see whether the relationship is healthy first.

6. She needs to be on the lookout for any obvious narcissistic traits in the prospective friend. If there is anything about the person that reminds her of her previous partner, she needs to back away. Interestingly, if the woman has really developed a good understanding of the traits of unhealthy people, she will start to observe this automatically.

7. She also needs to look back at some of the early warning signs in her previous relationships and pay more attention to those in the future. These include being wary of someone who comes across as too interested in the beginning, someone who wants to dominate her time, or someone who is jealous of her other relationships.

8. She needs to ask herself whether the new person builds her up or brings her down. She needs to be aware of her feelings and trust those feelings when it comes to future relationships.

9. In terms of her future relationships with men, she also needs to rethink how important physical appearance really is. Many narcissistic males are good looking, and she may have been caught up initially in the drama and excitement of how the man looked rather than focusing on his personality.

10. Finally, the woman needs to hold back from entering a new relationship until she feels content in her single state. It is important that she not be tempted to enter a new relationship, or return to the previous abusive one, out of financial insecurity. She needs to work at getting herself financially as independent as possible in order that financial concerns do not override her need for emotional security. Exploring other avenues of financial assistance or child care can protect her from making a decision that she will later regret. Also, a woman who is desperate to be in a relationship will not make good decisions, and so it is important that she give herself time to realize that she doesn't need a partner for her life to be complete. If, after a time of being on her own and being able to learn from her past experiences, she wants to have a new relationship, then I would encourage her to pursue it. Keeping in mind that all relationships require work, I would review with her some additional steps needed to make sure that a prospective new partner had a healthy personality.

Unfortunately, many women base their opinions of a new partner on how he treats them in the early stages of dating. However, these early interactions are typically in low-stress, pleasant environments with others not present and so do not give a true picture of his personality. Most individuals, including the narcissists, are able to present themselves in a positive light in such situations. But a woman needs to ascertain the person's emotional health early in the relationship before allowing herself to become emotionally involved. I would often tell the woman that she needed to be like a detective, finding clues as to whether a prospective partner was healthy by asking the following questions and observing the man in a variety of different settings.

1. Has he worked for the same company for most of his work life, or is he always changing jobs? Does he enjoy his work? Does he speak positively about his boss and work environment?

2. If previously married, does he have a respectful relationship with his ex-wife, such that they can attend events together when necessary? How often does he see his adult children or grandchildren? Does he have a good relationship with his own parents and siblings?

3. Does he maintain a healthy lifestyle (not using drugs or smoking, eating healthy foods, and exercising)?

4. Is he engaged in hobbies or sports? Is he reaching out to his community by being involved in a church, charitable organization, or club?

5. Does he have good friends that he sees frequently and can call on in an emergency? Do these friends seem to be supportive of him, and vice versa?

6. Is he generally a positive, happy person with a good sense of humor and able to laugh at himself?

7. Does he display a kind, respectful, and humble attitude?

8. Is he open to new ideas and respectful of differing opinions?

9. Does he have a strong faith in God that translates into helping others? Is he respectful of your religious beliefs?

10. Is he a good listener?

It is obvious that in order to answer yes to these questions, the woman needs to also be prepared to talk about herself rather than simply listening to the man. Many women are good listeners, but they need to be assertive in this area in order to discover how the man responds when they are the ones talking or voicing opinions that may differ from his.

In most cases, the man will have had at least one other prior relationship (possibly more), and it is important for the woman to find out why that ended and whether the man is prepared to take at least some of the responsibility for the breakup.

If the woman asks the question, "So why did your previous relationship end?" and the man replies, "I have no idea; it just came out of the blue," that is not a good sign. He may have been oblivious to the fact that his previous partner was unhappy. Even if his previous relationship failed because his wife was having an affair, he needs to be able to take some of the responsibility for it ending. A man who blames everything on his previous partner is likely going to repeat that behaviour. Also, if the man remains puzzled as to what went wrong in his previous relationship, it does not bode well for his ability to understand relationships and learn from experience. There should be some indication that the man is making the changes necessary to ensure that history does not repeat itself.

In addition to asking the various questions noted above, the woman needs to sharpen her observation skills. How he treats other people (e.g., waiters in restaurants and storekeepers) gives a clearer picture of his true personality. This is why it is important that the woman see a prospective mate interact with other people—so she can observe how he treats them. Seeing him together with other family members will offer a glimpse as to how he will likely treat her in the future. Typically, I would review all these strategies on how to choose a healthy partner before the woman began dating again. I would also remind the woman that she should also be able to answer yes to these questions herself as an indication of her own emotional health.

For some women, the stress and burden of being in an abusive relationship is such that they have no wish to repeat that experience. They may decide to devote themselves to their families or careers or volunteer work. And these also are healthy alternatives. The key is that at the end of the sessions the woman feels that she has the tools she needs to make healthy choices for herself going forward. These include choices regarding a potential partner, friends, and an employer.

When a woman I was counselling was able to report that she was feeling empowered in her family relationships, friendships, workplace, and church, then we would begin to wind down the sessions. In most cases, the decision to terminate counselling was a mutual one, as the woman would report that she had the knowledge and tools to interact differently with the unhealthy people in her life and to make healthy choices in the future.

I would reinforce with her how proud I was of the progress that she had made. I would also share with her that watching God work in her life to bring her to this point was an amazing blessing for me that brought me great joy.

Toward the end of our sessions, I met with Marie one last time to go over the gains she had made and whether she was ready to terminate counselling. I began by asking her to tell me how she was feeling about her relationship with Steve.

⚜

"Actually," Marie said, "I am excited to tell you that practising my assertive skills with Steve seems to be working."

"In what way?" I asked her.

"Well, for starters, as I mentioned before, when Steve starts to hassle me or get really rude, I just hand baby Stevie to him and say, "Here is your son. I am going for a little walk, and hopefully when I return you will be in a better mood." I think perhaps he thought it was a one-time thing, but the next time I stayed out even longer, and he had to call his mom for help. I thought she would criticize me, but surprisingly she told him he needed to treat me better. The other day, I could tell he was starting to get frustrated with me, but he just bit his tongue and said he needed to go for a walk, and that calmed him down. I told him I was impressed that he was making more of an attempt to manage his moods.

"The meals have worked out well too. When I first told him that we would be making our own suppers, I don't think he believed me, but I just fried up an egg and took Stevie up to bed. There wasn't very much in the fridge, because I hadn't gone shopping, so I think he had to settle for a peanut butter sandwich. After that, I noticed that he checks the fridge on Fridays, and if there isn't something he likes, he will pick something up at the grocery store. He is not a great cook, so he just buys those TV dinners, but that's fine with me. It is nice to have one night off from cooking.

"Remember how I told you that he was going over to his mom's place for supper several times a week? Well, I told him that was fine, but I also said I wanted him to bring me back some leftovers so I wouldn't have to cook that night either. And I phoned his mom to tell her how wonderful the food was. She has been much nicer to me and now makes sure that she makes enough for me as well. I am always very thankful to her, and I think she feels that perhaps cooking is her area of expertise and is happy to share. A few times she has even dropped over to see us. I make a big deal out of how much I think Stevie resembles Steve. She doesn't want to be called Grandma, as she says it makes her feel old, so we call her Baba instead."

"What about your own parents?" I asked.

"Well, that has really improved as well. I finally had the courage to sit down with my mom and have a heart-to-heart talk. I told her I didn't understand why she was reluctant to come over after Stevie was born, and she admitted that my dad wouldn't take the time to drive her. Remember how we talked about my dad having narcissistic traits? Well, it was really confirmed talking to my mom. She is almost afraid of him, and so I told her that either Steve or I will come and pick her up when Dad plays golf and she can spend time with Stevie then. She was nervous about telling Dad the plan, but we did it that same night.

"I remember that we talked about finding a way to validate him, so I started by reminding my dad about how close he was to his grandmother and how that gave him such a good start in life. I told him I was sure that he would want that same thing for Stevie (which he couldn't deny), and then I said that either Steve or I would pick up Mom and drive her to our place while he was golfing. I reminded him that on those days, he could always have supper with his golf buddies at the club and not have to worry about being home in time for supper, and he thought that was a good idea. I also said that I knew that little Stevie would one day appreciate the time with his grandmother the way my dad had enjoyed the time with his. He seemed pleased, almost as if it was his idea, and of course it didn't involve him putting himself out at all, so that made it easier for him to agree.

"Mom was so thrilled after we talked with Dad, and I realized that she is a really underassertive person, so I have been coaching her, and I bought her a copy of that book you loaned me to read as well. I think that when she saw me stand up to my dad and explain that this was our plan, she saw that it worked. She is so happy spending time with Stevie, and it gives me more time to work on my business."

"You said that both Steve and your dad criticized interior decorating as a career. Have they been better about that?" I asked.

"Absolutely," Marie replied. "Steve didn't want to admit it at first, but my business is really growing, and when he saw the extra money come in, I think he finally realized it was a good option for me. I even overheard him bragging about me to my dad, which blew me away.

"I did have a run-in with a client recently, as I had provided sketches with the idea that he would hire me to do the job myself. What happened was that he took the sketches and then told me he was going to do it himself after all. When he didn't pay me what I asked, I was assertive and told him that I would go to small claims court, and I think he was surprised at that. He decided that he would hire me anyway. But I told him he could just pay me for the sketches, because I just didn't have a good feeling about going forward with him. You were right about us HSPs having a good sense of other people, and I went with my instincts. Later I found out he had done the same thing to another decorator, so I was glad I trusted my feelings and got out before I lost money. Also Steve was impressed with how I dealt with the situation."

"So it sounds like things have improved enough with Steve that you are happier in the marriage?"

"Yes, I feel so much more at ease now knowing that I can handle Steve's outbursts by walking away. I don't take what he says personally like I used to do, because I know he would be this way with whoever he married. I try to praise him when he is being a good partner, and I just avoid him if he is in one of his moods. He has discovered that if I leave, it is more work for him, so he is really making an effort.

"He and my mom are starting to talk a little more. She told me that Steve reminded her too much of my dad when she first met him. She said she felt guilty that I was marrying someone like my dad and feared that I would end up making the same mistakes that she did. That was one of the reasons she stayed away in the early days. But I explained to her that I am my own person and I can handle Steve. Besides, between Stevie and my business, life is pretty busy.

"Oh, I must tell you I also made a new friend. Pattie is a little older than me and is a widow who lives next door. She loves Stevie and will come over and give me a break whenever I need one. She had a difficult husband who recently died, and so we have a lot in common. You were right that I don't need a lot of friends, and I am content with Pattie and my mom as friends.

"Oh, I almost forgot to tell you that one of the other things that has really improved is our sex life. I had tried leaving that book by John Gray on his bedside table, but he never mentioned it. Finally, I said that I was having trouble explaining to him some different things that I would really like. I told him that I wanted to read to him from the book so he would understand me better. He was really open to that, and I think he had been embarrassed to talk to me about the book. Anyway, sex has been much better since I spelled out for him the things he does that please me plus some new things he could try. Now it is not a chore but something that we can bond over. It turns out it is an area that he is pretty skilled at, and I can honestly boost his ego in that department."

"That sounds wonderful, Marie," I said. "Do you feel ready to end our sessions?"

"Yes, I do," she replied. "I learned a lot, and I have been practising all the things that you told me to do. Sometimes when I feel stressed, I can hear your voice in my head telling me that it is okay and I can handle it. It is almost as if I am a different person now. I am happier and more content, and I know that if a situation arises, I have the skills to handle it. I just wanted to ask you if I could contact you again if something came up in the future?"

"Of course, Marie," I replied. "I would be happy to see you again should the need arise. I am really confident that you will be able to handle things going forward without my help. I am so proud of you for taking the new information that you have learned and actually putting it into practice. But sometimes my clients come in for a 'tune-up,' as one woman called it. My door is always open figuratively, if not literally."

⟐

Now let's catch up with Stella, whose marriage was much more troubled than Marie's.

⟐

"Stella, you are looking much happier today," I said as she walked into my office.

"Well, I am pleased to report that Alex signed the separation agreement and agreed not to touch my pension if I signed over my half of the house to him. It turns out that my sister was a big influence in that department. She always told me that she envied our home, as she could only afford to rent an apartment, and now she sees herself and Alex having this nice home.

"I think she persuaded Alex to sign the agreement so she can move into our home with him, but I am just so glad he won't go after my pension now.

"At this stage in my life, I am okay with just renting. Any extra money I make I can put towards my retirement or maybe even doing a little travelling. It was nice to have a house, but I'm not that attached to material things, and having a house is a big responsibility. I think my sister will discover that Alex is not handy, plus he never wanted to do anything around the house. If it hadn't been for my neighbours, I wouldn't have managed. They were always so good to come over and help. I think they knew that Alex never did anything, but they never said anything. I just don't see them continuing to help out if it is just Alex, as they always seemed uncomfortable around him. I think they probably knew about his affairs too.

"I am getting settled in with my friend in her basement apartment, and she has invited me to come with her to her church, where I feel I can make a fresh start. It would be hard for me to see Alex and my sister sitting together in the pew, so I wanted to move to another church anyway. I really don't have to see Alex that often except for when our kids graduate, and I am okay with that. I expect that now that Alex is with my sister, he will probably not see my daughter as much, and that will be hard for her, but I don't say anything. She will discover his limitations for herself, unfortunately, and I will be there for her when he disappoints her in the future.

"What about your job, Stella? Are you happy there?"

"Yes, I am. My old boss was terrible, always trying to grab at me or staring at me, and I never knew what to do. I finally got up the courage to report him to HR, and he was livid. He tore a strip off me and said that he would get back at me for lying about him. But then three other women decided to report him as well, and so the company decided to move him to another location where he would only be working with males.

"The new boss is one of the women he was sexually abusing, and she is really nice and supportive, and the whole atmosphere of the office has changed for the better. Best of all, I got a raise, so that was a special bonus. God has really protected me throughout this whole time, and I feel like I am starting a new life without Alex always bringing me down.

"Funnily enough, Alex and I bought our burial plots together years ago, so I guess we will be reunited after death, because he doesn't want to buy me out and I don't care if I am buried beside him. I guess my sister may have something to say about that when she finds out, but it's not something I am worried about. I appreciate what you told me about using humour to get through the tough times."

"I am so happy for you, Stella," I said. "I believe you are ready to graduate, as you have put into practice the things that I have been sharing with you. I wish you every blessing in your new life."

Because of my Christian faith, I always asked the woman I was working with for permission to end each session by praying for her, whether she was Christian or not. I used the opportunity when I prayed in each session to summarize what we had focused on in the session, and I asked God to help the woman to remember that she was a beloved child of God and could move forward believing that God would help her to overcome her legacy of abuse.

At the termination of our counselling sessions, in my prayers, I also thanked God for giving me the opportunity of walking beside her while He opened her eyes to new ways of thinking and feeling about herself, leading to a new sense of freedom. I would commend her for the work that she had done and praise her for putting into practice what she had learned. In all my prayers, I was acutely aware of my own limitations in doing this work and that any help I could provide these women was achieved only through God.

In Conclusion

F inally, I would like to reiterate that I believe that my approach
to counselling as set forth in this guide is not a complicated
one, nor does it require the years of training that I myself engaged
in. This step-by-step guide takes advantage of the many helpful
educational resources already out there. Over the years, it has been
my great privilege to see women who were stressed, anxious, or
depressed get to a point where many of the presenting symptoms
were resolved. In life it is not usually the jobs we do that bring us
stress but our relationships with the people in our lives.

This approach is not applicable to all problems, of course, but
rather to a subset of individuals (many of them highly sensitive
women) who are in emotionally abusive relationships with men
with disordered personalities. If counsellors can help these abused
women to better understand themselves and what they are up
against, then they will be better prepared to make changes that
will give them a sense of freedom even if they choose to remain
in difficult relationships. If they experience us as loving, caring
guides, then God can enable them to embrace a new-found sense

of freedom and joy in their lives. Watching abused women move from being a survivor into true freedom has been one of the most gratifying experiences of my career, and my hope is that in sharing this guide more counsellors will be able to help these wonderful women.

Bibliography

Allerti, Robert, and Michael Emmons. *Your Perfect Right.* 10th edition. Oakland, CA: New Harbinger Publishers, 2017.

American Psychiatric Association. *Diagnostic and Statistical Manual of Mental Disorders.* 5th edition. Washington, DC: American Psychiatric Association Publishing, 2013.

Aron, Elaine. *The Highly Sensitive Person.* 25th anniversary edition. London: Kensington, 2020.

Bible, *New International Version.* Grand Rapids; MI: Zondervan, 1991.

Bourne, Edmund J. *The Anxiety and Phobia Workbook.* 7th edition. Oakland, CA: New Harbinger Publications, 2020.

Bristow, John Temple. *What Paul Really Said about Women.* San Francisco: Harper Collins Publishers, 1988

Cloud, Henry, and John Townsend. *Boundaries.* Grand Rapids, MI: Zondervan, 2017.

Donnelly, Michelle. *Safe Haven.* McMinnville, TN: Testimony Media Group, 2022.

Evans, Patricia. *The Verbally Abusive Relationship*. Avon, MA: Adams Media Corporation, 2010.

Forward, Susan. *Toxic Parents*. New York: Random House, 2002.

Grey, John. *Mars and Venus in the Bedroom*. New York: Harper Collins, 1997.

Johnson, David, and Jeff Van Vonderen. *The Subtle Power of Spiritual Abuse*. Minneapolis MN: Bethany House Publishers, 2005.

Landorf, Joyce. *Irregular People*. Waco, TX: Word Books, 1982.

McBride, Karyl. *Will I Ever Be Good Enough*. New York: Free Press, 2008.

Peck, Scott. *People of the Lie*. Chicago: Touchstone, 1998.

Peterson, Eugene. *The Message//Remix: The Bible in Contemporary Language*. Colorado Springs, CO: Nav Press, 2003.

About The Author

D r. Laraine Birnie is a Ph.D. clinical psychologist who has
worked in inpatient, outpatient and family court clinic settings
in Canada and Jamaica. She was chief psychologist at a psychiatric
rehabilitation center and appeared as an expert witness in family
court regarding child custody cases. She spent 3 years as assistant
professor of psychology at Mount Saint Vincent University in Nova
Scotia. In addition to being a guest lecturer at Acadia Divinity
School, she has given workshops and provided consultations to
pastors, churches and other Christian groups in Nova Scotia. She
has also led women's bible study groups for many years. She has
worked in private practice for almost three decades with women
suffering from emotional and psychological abuse. This book is a
culmination of the strategies she developed working with those
women. Dr. Birnie is the mother of two cherished daughters
(Sarah and Carolyn) both psychologists, and five grandchildren
(Owen and Miles in Halifax and Mira, Nathan and Noelle in
Ottawa. Her children's book, *The Adventures of A, B, and C* was
published in 2023 as a gift to them.

Printed in the United States
by Baker & Taylor Publisher Services